Cambridge Elements

COLLECTIVE RESISTANCE TO NEOLIBERALISM

Paul Almeida
University of California, Merced
Amalia Pérez Martín
University of California, Merced

CAMBRIDGE
UNIVERSITY PRESS

University Printing House, Cambridge CB2 8BS, United Kingdom

One Liberty Plaza, 20th Floor, New York, NY 10006, USA

477 Williamstown Road, Port Melbourne, VIC 3207, Australia

314–321, 3rd Floor, Plot 3, Splendor Forum, Jasola District Centre, New Delhi – 110025, India

103 Penang Road, #05–06/07, Visioncrest Commercial, Singapore 238467

Cambridge University Press is part of the University of Cambridge.

It furthers the University's mission by disseminating knowledge in the pursuit of education, learning, and research at the highest international levels of excellence.

www.cambridge.org
Information on this title: www.cambridge.org/9781108969932
DOI: 10.1017/9781108980005

First published 2022

A catalogue record for this publication is available from the British Library.

ISBN 978-1-108-96993-2 Paperback
ISSN 2633-3570 (online)
ISSN 2633-3562 (print)

Collective Resistance to Neoliberalism

Elements in Contentious Politics

DOI: 10.1017/9781108980005
First published online: August 2022

Paul Almeida
University of California, Merced

Amalia Pérez Martín
University of California, Merced

Author for correspondence: Paul Almeida, palmeida@ucmerced.edu

Abstract: Civil society actors have contested the fifty-year-long transition to a global economy based on the principles of neoliberalism. Mobilization against neoliberal measures represents one of the most common forms of social movement activity across the world. We explore the evolution of resistance to economic liberalization from the 1970s to the current period. Our study highlights several dimensions of civic opposition to the implementation of free market policies, including: forms of neoliberalism; geographic distribution of protest events across world regions and time; and outcomes of movement campaigns.

Keywords: austerity, social movements, privatization, protest, threat

ISBNs: 9781108969932 (PB), 9781108980005 (OC)
ISSNs: 2633-3570 (online), 2633-3562 (print)

Contents

1 Resistance to Neoliberalism

Introduction

Between November 2020 and March 2021, hundreds of thousands of farmers from India's northern states marched and laid siege to the periphery of New Delhi in a massive sit-in and encampment on the arterial highways. The farmers directed their protests, with a prominent presence of women, against the deregulation of agricultural commodity prices and related policies and demanded a minimum price for their products. India's major labor unions joined in a one-day solidarity strike against the measures with an estimated 250 million workers participating. A few months earlier, Prime Minister Narendra Modi and his Bharatiya Janata Party (BJP) had passed three laws in Parliament that swiftly overturned legislation protecting rural producers that had been enacted in 1955 at the height of state-led development in the global South (Narayanan, 2020; Waghre, 2021). The dramatic actions in India represent the highest level of nation-based collective resistance to neoliberalism to date. In late 2021, after a year of permanent protest encampments and regional electoral losses, Prime Minister Modi announced he would repeal the farm laws.

In Chile, in a ten-week period between mid-October and December 2019, collective actors produced more than 3,300 protest events, with street marches reaching up to one million participants – the largest outpouring of mass dissent in decades (Somma et al., 2020). The *estallido social* also resulted in twenty deaths and thousands of injured citizens in the face of police repression (Somma et al., 2021). While sudden price hikes in public transportation triggered the initial uprising, the most frequent protests in the following weeks were over the weakening of the welfare state, with demands for more health care, educational access, housing, general social provisions (Somma et al., 2021) and, as also occurred in India, denouncements of the abuses of repressive forces (Godinez Galay and Binder, 2021). The Chileans' demands for expanded social citizenship rights appear especially striking given that for decades Chile has served as the exemplar for successful market reforms in the developing world (Harvey, 2005). The mass uprising also resulted in new elections for a Constituent Assembly in 2021, where left-of-center parties and new social movement constituencies performed exceedingly well. The year ended with the victory of the progressive Social Convergence coalition in the presidential elections.

The historic protests in India and Chile vividly demonstrate the ongoing resistance to neoliberalism across the globe. These large-scale campaigns also contain many of the components of collective action discussed in the pages that follow. We examine the dynamics of various forms of economic threats, organizational fields and infrastructures, disruptive repertoires of contention, and the political consequences of mobilized opposition to neoliberalism. These collective challenges remain relevant as policy analysts forecast increasing economic austerity by governments across the globe through 2025 (Ortiz and Cummins, 2021).

Civil society actors have contested the fifty-year-long transition to a global economy based on the principles of deregulation, free trade, and a deepening market society. Scholars and activists alike generally refer to these principles as the doctrine of *neoliberalism*. Given the pervasiveness of market-driven reforms, mobilization against neoliberal measures represents one of the most common forms of social movement activity across the world. Most recently, in 2019, a new wave of economic-based uprisings occurred in Chile, Ecuador, France, Honduras, Iraq, Iran, Lebanon, South Africa, and Sudan.[1] Even in the midst of the global coronavirus pandemic between 2020 and 2022, massive popular protest campaigns against economic policies erupted in Ecuador, Costa Rica, Colombia, Cuba, Kazakhstan, Panama, Sri Lanka, Sudan, and India. Several of the recent campaigns broke national records for their size and scale. We explore the evolution of resistance to economic liberalization from the 1970s through the first two decades of the twenty-first century. The study highlights massive civic opposition to the implementation of free market policies in multiple arenas, including: specific economic policies that drive collective action; geographic distribution of major protest events across localities, world regions, and time; composition of protest coalitions; and the outcomes of movement campaigns.

The *economic context* of mobilization, especially in terms of various forms of trade, market regulation, and state-capital relations, has been de-emphasized in extant social movement studies. The most influential works that incorporate political economy into movement analyses tend to use broad neo-Polanyist frameworks of the "double-movement" as a counter to unfettered forms of market society (Roberts, 2008; Silva, 2009). Since neoliberalism operates at the global level as the dominant economic formation, and mass mobilization is often triggered directly or indirectly by its specific policies, a sustained focus on the economic drivers of protest and popular unrest offers huge payoffs to our understanding of social movements across multiple continents and over time.

Defining Neoliberalism: What are the Popular Sectors Contesting?

Neoliberalism is a set of economic policies with political, ideological, and cultural components. Understanding these components helps us to better

[1] See, www.ucpress.edu/blog/47494/the-global-protests-of-october-2019/.

specify the conditions and the context that eventuate in collective struggles against neoliberalism. The term emerged from classical liberalism, a period of unregulated capitalism between the 1830s and 1930s (Polanyi, 1944). This was the epoch whereby governments swept away the last vestiges of feudal laws protecting vulnerable populations from an emerging market society in Europe (Markoff, 1996). Classical liberalism met its demise with the onset of the Great Depression of the 1930s. The period was followed by state intervention in economic planning and a rapid expansion of the welfare state between the 1930s and 1970s (including labor protections). In the affluent nations of the global North, these decades are known as the era of Keynesianism, for the state-interventionist economic policies associated with the British economist, John Maynard Keynes. In lower- and middle-income countries of the global South, the mid-twentieth century is referred to as the period of state-led development. The reemergence of deregulation in the 1970s and 1980s by national, regional, and local governments institutionalized a new round of economic liberalism commonly known as *neoliberalism*. Since neoliberalism has become such a buzzword in the twenty-first century (especially for its critics), it is essential to more precisely define its usage and separate the multidimensional concept from other practices and economic policies.

Economic Dimension: The "neo" component emphasizes that neoliberalism is a revised version of the classical liberal doctrine that emerged in the nineteenth century. This new economic liberalism had to be adjusted to fit a context characterized by economic and political actors that did not exist under classical liberalism such as transnational firms with monopoly powers, and democratic states with commitments to social welfare (Evans and Sewell, 2013; Mann, 2012a; Brenner et al., 2010). Neoliberalism encompasses a set of market-based economic policies, including the privatization of public infrastructure and services, dismantling of social welfare apparatuses, reduced controls on capital transfers and investments, deregulation of credit and labor markets, free trade agreements, structural adjustment mandated by international financial institutions (IFIs), fiscal austerity, and new regimes of intellectual property (Prasad, 2006). All of these components transform the relationship between citizens and the state. This ample range of policy prescriptions came to be known as the "Washington Consensus" in the late 1980s and early 1990s (Williamson, 1993). The IFIs and a growing number of state managers considered the Washington Consensus policies as the "best practice" for developing economies (Fourcade-Gourinchas and Babb, 2002; Evans and Sewell, 2013). Also, the expansion of the financial services sector (i.e., financialization) opened new areas for capitalist profit-making (Krippner, 2011; Brown, 2015: 70–72). Along with financialization (Prechel and Berkowitz, 2020), increased globalization of economic activity, technological changes, and international investment booms have also been salient features of the neoliberal era (Dicken, 2015; Almeida and Chase-Dunn, 2018).

Market fundamentalism has decreased the power of organized labor and intensified income inequality (Moody, 1997; Piketty, 2014). In this line of analysis, scholars locate the shift from welfare to "workfare" under neoliberalism as one of the major indicators of increased commodification or contractualization processes in multiple realms of social life (Standing, 2011; Reese, 2011). These practices, when applied to employment, are referred to as *labor flexibility*. Standing (2011) contends that neoliberalism has produced a new global class, the "precariat," characterized by limited employment-related security. Large segments of the population are vulnerable to precarity, but some groups are more exposed than others, especially youth, women, the elderly, immigrants, and racialized populations (Canizales, 2021).

Political Dimension: A comprehensive or thick sociological explanation of neoliberalism should go beyond its economic definition and incorporate the power of states. A more globalized world is not one in which markets have been freed from politics or governments. At the transnational level, powerful states in the world system continue to engage in efforts to gain political and economic control over other countries by political and military means (Evans and Sewell, 2013). Neoliberalism is a transnational political project aspiring to reconstruct from above the relationships between the market, the state, and social citizenship (Robinson, 2014). As Polanyi (1944) noted, there is no market freedom without a state that regulates and reproduces it. The centrality of state actors in diffusing market fundamentalism shows that neoliberalism is not simply anti-statist (Bockman, 2013; Brown, 2015).

Another component of the political dimension of neoliberalism is the global growth of a proactive penal or carceral state (Wacquant, 2009). With economies more focused on precarious labor markets, mass unemployment, labor union decline, and flexible labor contracts, huge swathes of the population fall into pockets of economic insecurity. One response from wealthier states is to control low-income and precarious populations with punitive laws that lead to mass incarceration (Flores, 2018) and mass deportation (Golash-Boza, 2015).

The politics of mass incarceration can be viewed as the repressive side of neoliberalism, even in democratic states (Cobbina, 2019; Flores, 2018). This remaking of the state encompasses the combination of restrictive "workfare" with an expansive "prisonfare" aiming to discipline the precariat. Through this double social-penal regulation the state reasserts its responsibility and potency in crime management, while simultaneously failing to enact market restrictions to protect social citizenship rights and the environment (Gilmore, 2007). In this conception, the neoliberal state regulates social insecurity and deepening inequality through "a carceral big government" historically driven in the United States not by trends in criminality, but by the class and racial backlash against progressive social policies advocated by the social movements of the 1960s and 1970s (Alexander, 2010; Davis, 2003). These "made in the USA" penal measures and policies devised during the "war on crime" in the 1980s and 1990s have been widely diffused, not without variations, across Western Europe (Wacquant, 2009) and the world. According to Robinson (2020), the "global police state" is centrally aimed at coercive exclusion of surplus humanity through social control and militarized accumulation. It expresses itself not only through mass incarceration, but also as racist police violence and paramilitary repression against social movements, US-led drug wars in Latin America, the Chinese high-tech systems of mass surveillance, the persecution of immigrants and refugees, and the repression of environmental justice activists opposing extractive industries and agribusinesses, among many others.

The active recourse to law-and-order mechanisms as a regular feature of neoliberalism to exercise control over marginalized social groups and generate subordination (Auyero et al., 2015; De Giorgi, 2017) leads to the formation of a "centaur state" (Wacquant, 2009). Such a government shows drastically different faces at the two ends of the social hierarchy: liberal and permissive toward the middle and upper classes, and authoritarian toward the lower classes. Traditional political parties representing the right to the center-left have also converged on this two-pronged strategy of promoting neoliberal economic policies combined with punitive laws against the racialized poor. For example, in the mid-1990s, former US president Bill Clinton championed North American free trade while simultaneously enacting harsh crime and immigration legislation. Indeed, by the 1980s even social democratic parties across the global North abandoned Keynesianism, and came under the influence of market-oriented economists to shift their policy platforms along neoliberal lines (Mudge, 2018). In most cases of economically induced collective action, it is the political dimension that oppositional groups directly confront. More specifically, collective action coalesces around a particular neoliberal policy enacted by a local or national government and the state becomes the final arbiter in implementing the measure or not (e.g., protest campaigns against privatization, free trade, and austerity).

Ideological and Cultural Dimension: Scholars who emphasize the ideational and cultural components of neoliberalism reject the notion of "neoliberal inevitability" – i.e., neoliberalism as a product of natural law, economic evolution, or some other inescapable historical mechanism (Burridge and Markoff, 2022). In this respect, market fundamentalism has become "the prevailing ideational regime" (Somers, 2008: 2) and "common sense" in the current era (Brown, 2015: 35). These sentiments strengthened over time as Keynesianism faded to the distant past.

The ideational hegemony of neoliberal culture has flourished within expert and academic communities, government policy circles (Markoff and Montecinos, 1993; Mudge, 2018), and popular culture (Centeno and Cohen, 2012). Neoliberal ideological dominance arises from institutional changes occurring through national and transnational interest groups and advocacy networks of experts and think tanks (Peck, 2010; Bockman and Eyal, 2002; Kentikelenis and Babb, 2019). Moreover, in policy and government circles, a "rhetoric of reaction" has been established (Centeno and Cohen, 2012). This means that policy shifts away from market logic are deemed to result in perverse outcomes and systemic dangers. Indeed, the "perverse thesis" that welfare regimes produce poverty and a culture of dependency is one of neoliberalism's most successful ideational schemes (Somers, 2008: 80). The IFIs also subscribe to and promote this type of market fundamentalism (Babb and Kentikelenis, 2021).

As a form of popular culture, neoliberalism promotes individualism (Evans and Sewell, 2013; Harvey, 2005). Individual responsibility becomes a central vocabulary of motive for the construction of an entrepreneur self, the spread of markets, and the legitimization for intensified competition. For our purposes, the focus on individualism and heightened consumerism would appear to present substantial obstacles for collective action, especially with the weakening of traditional actors in the interorganizational field of civil society, and what others arguably claim is an overall decline in social capital and civic life (Sarracino and Mikucka, 2017). In summary, the political, ideological, and cultural dimensions of neoliberalism shape the specific economic policies generating collective resistance.

Economic Policy Drivers of Collective Action

One way scholars gain analytical leverage from the concept of neoliberalism involves focusing on specific policies or actions by states and international governing bodies. These include the economic policies of austerity, structural adjustment, privatization, and free trade.[2]

Austerity Policies: The earliest forms of neoliberalism encompassed austerity policies in the global North and were soon emulated in the global South. Starting with the global economic recession in the early 1970s, wealthier

[2] Intensified and less-regulated resource extraction could also be added to this list of economic policies driving anti-neoliberal collective action.

governments in the global North faced a "fiscal crisis of the state" (O'Connor, 1973). This came after two decades of unprecedented economic growth driven by Keynesian policies of state intervention and a massive expansion of the welfare state seeking full employment. Governments began to implement austerity programs across the industrialized capitalist world in the mid-1970s. Austerity policies centered on reducing budget deficits and public debt. Policymakers introduced a range of actions, including funding cuts to social services, budget reductions in public education, mass layoffs and wage freezes in the public sector, removal of government subsidies to basic consumption items, housing, and transportation, among many other cutbacks.

Structural Adjustment Programs: A set of neoliberal policies closely related to austerity, structural adjustment originates from the debt crisis in the global South that emerged in the early 1980s and continues to the present. The crisis began from a combination of massive foreign lending, falling commodity prices for global South exports, and rising interest rates. In 1970, global South governments owed $64 billion to foreign banks and governments. The global South debt grew to $686 billion in 1984 and then to $2.2 trillion in 2000 (Walton and Seddon, 1994; Robinson, 2004). At the end of 2020, the total external debt for low- and middle-income countries combined reached $8.7 trillion (World Bank, 2022). The IFIs, especially the International Monetary Fund (IMF) and World Bank, intervened to manage the crisis. The IFIs brokered negotiations between the governments of newly indebted countries and banks in the global North. They also negotiated future lines of credit, rescheduled debt payments, and reduced overall debt in exchange for the borrowing countries' willingness to adjust their national economic policymaking in a more unregulated fashion.

The adjustments to economies in Asia, Africa, Eastern Europe, the former Soviet Union, and Latin America came to be known as *structural adjustment agreements*. Global South governments signed agreements for debt rescheduling and relief in exchange for making deep changes to their national economies. The signed accords stipulated a number of measures to be undertaken (referred to as "conditionality"), such as: reducing state price controls and consumer subsidies; removal of import tariffs; a focus on export production, nontraditional agricultural crops, and foreign direct investment; labor flexibility; and many of the austerity policies discussed earlier in the global North. From 1955 to 1970, only six developing countries had signed such agreements with the World Bank and IMF. In the 1970s, about three countries per year entered into debt rescheduling. In the early 1980s, the number of debt reschedulings in the global South rose dramatically from twenty-three in 1981–2, to sixty-five in 1983–4 (Walton and Seddon, 1994: 13–17).

Between 1980 and mid-1995, structural adjustment largely included traditional austerity measures of wage freezes and subsidy cuts affecting the urban and rural popular classes. By the late 1990s, new structural adjustment agreements also included the *privatization* of substantial portions of the economic and public infrastructure. Between 1985 and 2014 alone, the IMF placed an astonishing 55,000 conditions on 133 countries (Kentikelenis et al., 2016). Figure 1 provides a global heat map of the intensity of IMF and World Bank conditionality from 1981 to 2020 by highlighting the number of years a country is under the influence of either the World Bank or IMF. As the heat map illustrates, it is largely the nations of the global South and Eastern Europe that have endured the external pressure to restructure their national economies in a market-oriented framework. Such a wide and homogenous push toward market reforms across multiple continents, goes far in explaining the isomorphism of neoliberal policymaking on a global level. It also assists in our understanding of the frequent outbreak of protest campaigns around the world challenging the measures.

Privatization Policies: Privatization has nearly become synonymous with neoliberalism. In the global North, privatization policies in Britain trace back to Thatcherism in the early 1980s with the selling off of state assets such as mines and railroads. In the global South, privatization emerged a decade later (with important exceptions such as the privatizations in Pinochet's Chile in the late 1970s). Some of the most common targets for privatization by IFIs, foreign investors, and local economic elites tied to transnational capital include: petroleum/natural gas reserves; water administration; electricity and power distribution; port management, public health care and pension systems (social security); telecommunications; and education. Most of these state institutions and assets came into existence in the early to mid-twentieth century at the height of state-led development, while public utilities were initially created in the late nineteenth century in the global North. At the end of economic liberalism in the late 1920s, with the onset of the Great Depression, national governments switched paths and began to take over strategic components of the economy.

In the global South, much of the twentieth century involved the state reclaiming institutions and natural resource reserves from colonial and neocolonial powers in Europe, Japan, and the United States. From the Mexican Revolution to anti-colonial struggles in Africa and Asia, political leaders focused on state administration and control over strategic industries and natural reserves. For instance, the nationalization of US-owned oil companies by the Cuban revolutionary government in 1960 heralded a wave of nationalizations and expropriations that occurred in Saudi Arabia, Libya, and Iran during the 1970s

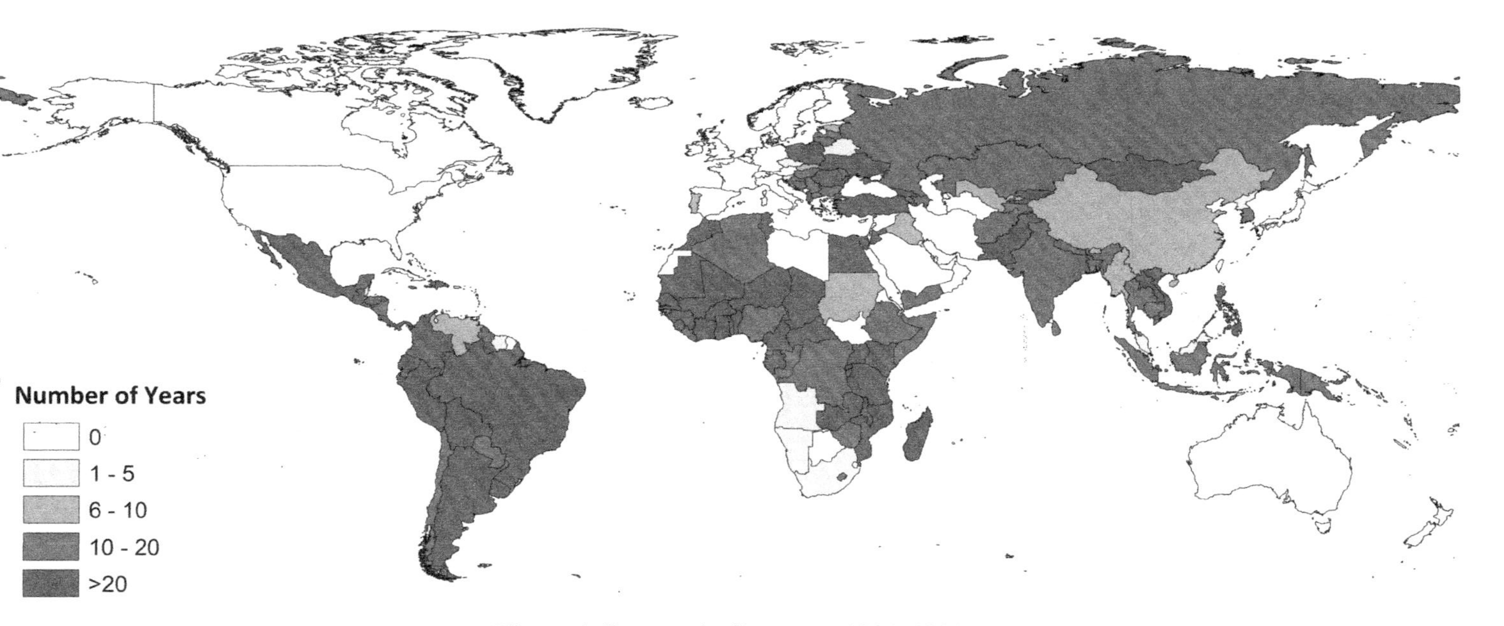

Figure 1 Structural adjustment, 1981–2020

Source: Created by the authors based on Abouharb and Cingranelli (2007), Abouharb and colleagues (2015), World Bank Development Policy Actions Data Base, and IMF Monitoring of Fund Arrangements Database (MONA).

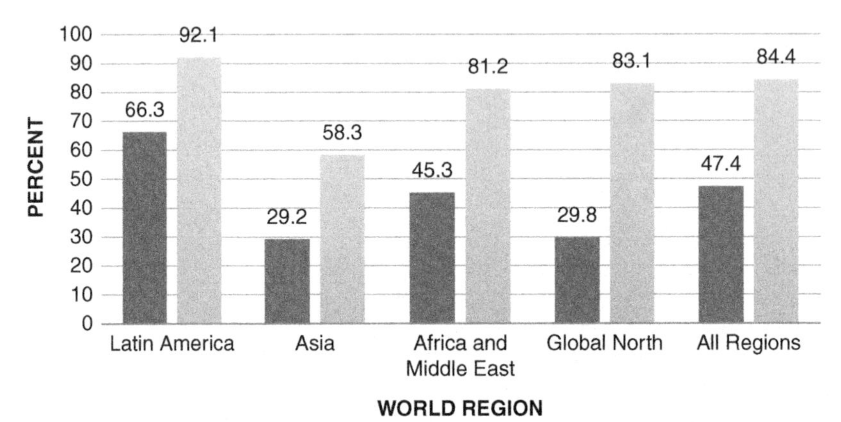

Figure 2 Labor strikes in firms undergoing privatization and unionization rates
Source: Created by the authors from data in Chong and López-de-Silanes (2005). Representative sample drawn from universe of 1,500 privatized firms.

(Pérez Martín, 2020). With the advent of the global debt crisis in the 1980s and 1990s, structural adjustment in conjunction with the ascendance of market fundamentalist thinking introduced privatization policies throughout the world. Privatization measures faced stiff popular opposition. Figure 2 illustrates the contested nature of privatization from a representative sample of 308 privatized industries and units between 1982 and 2000. Labor strikes occurred in nearly half of the units under privatization (47.4 percent), and these were public firms that were highly unionized in nearly all world regions.

Free Trade Treaties: Around the same time as the ascendance of privatization policies in the 1990s came international free trade agreements. Free trade agreements call for domestic deregulation of economic activities and greater openness to foreign investment. Some forms of regional free trade blocs are loosely governed at the supranational level such as the European Union, ASEAN, APEC, CAFTA, and NAFTA. The World Trade Organization (WTO) came into existence in 1996 to guide a global system of free trade (formerly known as General Agreement on Tariffs and Trade, GATT). Other free trade agreements are bilateral such as the United States' free trade agreements with South Korea, Peru, Panama, and Colombia. Some regional free trade attempts have been embroiled in conflict such as the Free Trade Area of the Americas (FTAA) and the Trans-Pacific Partnership (TPP) and failed to materialize as formal agreements (Ayres, 1998). Free trade treaties also facilitate greater foreign investment in the extraction industries.

Theoretical Perspectives on Popular Opposition to Neoliberalism

Opposition to neoliberalism begins with the notion of groups perceiving they will be made worse off if the state enacts a free market-type measure. Several concepts and processes from social movement theory are synthesized and combined in unique ways to assist in explaining the timing and scale of collective resistance to market-oriented reforms and the removal of social protections. The predominant factors driving anti-neoliberal mobilization include perceived economic threats, infringements on the moral economy, organizational infrastructures, and past collective action experience.

Economic Threat: In general, austerity and other neoliberal measures activate collective action by the perceived threat or loss in well-being for particular groups. Advances in collective action scholarship suggest that *losses* are more likely to produce mobilization than perceived gains (Tilly, 1978; Tversky and Kahneman, 1992; Snow et al., 1998; Bergstrand, 2014; Almeida, 2019a). This helps explain why austerity-type protests and campaigns against neoliberalism, at times, mushroom into such massive episodes and occur with regularity around the globe. The threat is either forthcoming or currently experienced (Goldstone and Tilly, 2001; Pinard, 2011; Meyer, 2021: 22). Forthcoming threats often involve such policies as impending privatization, labor flexibility laws, regressive taxation, and free trade treaties. In these scenarios, activists, organizers, and communities may take advantage of the time between when the legislation or decree is introduced and implemented. A campaign may emerge to try and impede the looming threat via mass mobilization before it becomes law or shortly thereafter. Other anti-neoliberal campaigns emerge from the suddenly imposed threats of price increases, wage freezes, or mass layoffs. These collective actions appear relatively more spontaneous.

The *scope* of the threat also matters (Zepeda-Millán, 2017). The larger the population impacted by the threat brings in a greater number of people and broader coalitions to the campaigns. National-level policies that negatively affect lower- and middle-income groups, such as subsidy removals and privatization of fundamental public goods of health care, education, water, and utilities, maintain the potential to trigger a major protest campaign. Threats to specific groups limited to certain geographical regions or occupational sectors may lead to more modest levels of mobilization. Economic threats also have a *moral economy dimension*. When economic actions by states break social norms and beliefs about maintaining social welfare or affirming social rights, they may lead to especially explosive episodes of collective action driven by moral outrage (Auyero, 2004; Simmons, 2016).

Organizational Fields and Coordinating Infrastructures: The organizational setting goes far in explaining if communities will act on neoliberal threats, and how forcefully. The organizational field is made up of a diversity of organizations, and the size and diversity of the field varies across time and space (Ray, 2000). The field includes civil society associations such as labor unions, community-based organizations (CBOs), nonprofit advocacy groups, nongovernmental organizations (NGOs), and social movement organizations (SMOs). The organizational field is also composed of everyday organizations such as schools, faith-based institutions, recreational and sports clubs, parent associations, and community groups such as choirs, gardening collectives, and reading circles. These everyday organizations can also be mobilized through block recruitment in anti-neoliberal campaigns. We explore variations in the organizational assets in the geographical distribution of dissent in Section 2, and their role in determining campaign outcomes in Section 3.

Arguably, internet communication technologies (ICTs) serve as the most critical coordinating structure of the twenty-first century (Castells, 2013). The new digital technologies greatly reduce the communication costs to produce large and more frequent collective actions (Tufekci, 2017). In the global North, these processes were observed in the late 1990s and 2000s with webpages and cellphones used in organizing national and transnational collective actions against free trade. Later in the 2000s and 2010s, SMS texting, Facebook, and Twitter played major roles in the largest mass mobilizations in the global North and South (e.g., Occupy Wall Street; Climate Justice; Indignados; Indian Farmers; anti-Austerity in Iraq, Iran, and Lebanon; Chilean youth; etc.). By the late 2010s and early 2020s, activists coordinated most of the major protest campaigns in the global South with the popular messaging platforms of WhatsApp, Signal, and Telegram (with WhatsApp as the dominant platform). Table 1 demonstrates the tremendous growth in access to ICTs in Latin America and the Caribbean between 2000 and 2016. Similar trends can be found in Africa and Asia in the same years. According to the World Bank, in East Asia and the Pacific the Internet audience grew from 5.6 percent to 53.2 percent of the population, while in the Middle East and North Africa the increase was from 2 percent to 47 percent. In Sub-Saharan Africa the Internet usage went from 0.5 percent to 19.37 percent of the total population. The capacity of civil society to mobilize against neoliberalism via ICTs has become such a powerful force that governments have shut down national internet/social media access at the height of economic-based protest campaigns in India, Iran, Iraq, Colombia, Kazakhstan, and Ecuador.

The coordinating function of ICTs does not replace traditional offline face-to-face organizing and capacity building (Tufekci, 2017). All of the elements

Table 1 Individuals using the Internet (% of population), Latin America and Caribbean

Country	2000	2016
Argentina	7	71
Bahamas	8	80
Barbados	4	80
Belize	6	45
Bolivia	1	40
Brazil	3	61
Chile	17	84
Colombia	2	58
Costa Rica	6	66
Cuba	1	43
Dominica	9	67
Domin. Repub.	4	64
Ecuador	1	54
El Salvador	1	29
Grenada	4	56
Guatemala	1	35
Guyana	7	36
Haiti	0	12
Honduras	1	30
Jamaica	3	44
Mexico	5	60
Nicaragua	1	25
Panama	7	54
Paraguay	1	53
Peru	3	45
Uruguay	11	66
Venezuela	3	60

Source: World Bank, International Statistics, 2019.

mentioned earlier in the organizational field provide capabilities *to sustain* strategic mobilization once collective action takes off, even for large events first coordinated online. Also, if economic threats do not subside or continue mounting, they provide the motivational interest to prolong a protest campaign originally synchronized by social media platforms. Nonetheless, ICTs provide an unprecedented jump in scale for collective action through mass, instantaneous, and relatively horizontal communication (Castells, 2013). The accelerated expansion of ICTs in the 2010s and 2020s in the global South substantially raises the "mobilization potential" (Klandermans, 1997) for resistance to neoliberalism and other threats.

Strategic Experience: Strategic experience brings in past encounters of mobilization against neoliberalism. Given that neoliberalism persists over several decades, many localities have multiple interactions with specific neoliberal policies and past mobilization. Just the failure or perceived growing hardship from previous rounds of neoliberalism makes communities wary of new rounds of policy implementation, and collective action more likely in the future. Especially forceful are past experiences *mobilizing against neoliberalism*. Those experiences deposit skill sets for organizing and frames for interpreting economic policy changes (Almeida et al., 2021). These previous collective actions greatly reduce the cost of mobilizing against neoliberalism in the present.

Basic Forms of Resistance

Resistance to neoliberalism often comes in the form of a particular level of collective action. These levels range from everyday forms of resistance to transnational movements.

Everyday resistance involves surreptitious acts by individuals in small groups to defend themselves. Such actions include work slowdowns, gossip, graffiti, symbolic gestures of defiance, and humming or singing prohibited songs (Scott, 1985; Johnston, 2005; Bayat, 2010). The most likely environments for these micro forms of resistance are extremely oppressive or exploitive settings. Larger forms of collective action become difficult to assemble in these repressive situations, hence subaltern groups use forms of noncooperation most suitable to their current existence. In the context of neoliberalism, these settings include export processing zones, immigration detention centers and prisons, and rural areas where conflicts occur over resource extraction and agro-exports.

Local grassroots movements appear similar to social movements in that they use commonplace tactics such as marches, rallies, petitions, and boycotts. Local movements mobilize against neoliberal policies *at the municipal or regional level*. The mobilizations are usually smaller and endure for less time than national campaigns. Often the mobilization may be over the privatization of a local utility such as water administration or cutbacks to city social and welfare services (Reese, 2011). The groups mobilizing focus on the local policy and tend to originate from the region in question. The campaigns against electricity privatization in Arequipa, Peru and water privatization in Cochabamba, Bolivia in the early 2000s provide emblematic cases of local grassroots movements resisting neoliberal policies (Arce, 2008).

National social movements involve large and sustained mobilizations that focus on the national government or large corporations in response to neoliberal threats. They are often composed of multiple organizations and use conventional and nonconventional tactics such as petitions, social media blasts, street marches, teach-ins, and organizing drives. Usually, a key group leads the mobilization (e.g., public sector workers) and then allies may join in the struggle. The most common contribution to collective action at the national level occurs when one or more preexisting national social movement forms part of the coalition battling against a major market reform such as a free trade treaty, IMF agreement, or national level privatization. Women's movements, indigenous people's movements, labor movements, and environmental movements (among several others) have bolstered national-level campaigns against market fundamentalism.

In more intensified conflicts over neoliberalism, protests may escalate into a *wave or cycle of protest*. Waves of protests last for multiple years and involve many social sectors covering much of the national territory (Tarrow, 1989). When a series of sequential campaigns take place over several neoliberal policies, the situation may convert into a wave of protest (e.g., Bolivia 2000–2005; Argentina 1997–2003; Greece 2010–15; Spain 2010–15). These waves deposit long-lasting and fungible resources that may be used for other forms of politics, including electoral mobilization (as we explore in Section 3). They also leave long lasting impressions and beliefs in the general population about neoliberal policymaking.

Transnational mobilization represents the most extensive form of anti-neoliberal collective action. Resistance can be defined as transnational when groups in multiple countries coordinate action against economic liberalization measures. Some of the most common forms of transnational mobilization are witnessed in the global economic justice movement that focuses on international free trade treaties and economic summits such as the World Social Forum (WSF) and Via Campesina (a global peasant/small farmer movement). The global economic justice movement reached an apex in the late 1990s and early 2000s with several campaigns mobilizing demonstrators in dozens of countries simultaneously in days of action against the WTO, G8, World Bank/IMF meetings, and other elite financial gatherings and summits (Wood, 2012).

Another level of collective action, often taken for granted in the literature, involves the *protest campaign*. Tilly (2004: 4) argues that "unlike a one-time petition, declaration, or mass meeting, a campaign extends beyond any single event." Campaigns mobilize individuals and groups in collective action over a limited period of time with relatively specific goals compared to a larger social movement (Marwell and Oliver, 1984). The campaign can occur at the local, regional, national, or transnational level. Many of the mobilization episodes against economic threats take the form of a protest campaign. A particularly powerful campaign (or a focal campaign) can create the conditions for long-term resistance to neoliberalism by providing the organizational and experiential basis of future campaigns. Campaigns against water privatization in Latin America tend to last between several weeks and several months, while campaigns against free trade can endure for multiple years, as in Costa Rica in the mid-2000s, and the wider Latin American region in the case of the Free Trade Area of the Americas (FTAA).

Methodological Approach

Multiple data sets and sources are employed in this study, including: 1) an original protest event data set of large-scale anti-neoliberal protest campaigns between 1970 and 2020; 2) protest event data at the subnational level in Mexico and Costa Rica; 3) transnational protest event data from activist websites; and 4) comparative campaign and election data from secondary sources and field research in Latin America. We collected data on the largest protest campaigns against neoliberalism on a global scale between 1970 and 2020 coded from Nexis Uni, Global NewsBank, SCAD, and PRIO news sources and protest listings. To be included in our data set, a protest campaign required 100,000 or more participants or to occur on a national scale in multiple cities. The protest campaign also had to be primarily focused on a major issue related to neoliberal policy: austerity measures, price increases, privatization, free trade, or a combination of two or more policies. In total we identified 915 major protest campaigns. No large-scale protest campaign was identified between 1970 and 1974 in the news repositories consulted. We refer to this data set as the Large-Scale Anti-Neoliberal Protest Data Base. By standardizing our data across only large-scale campaigns we capture *the general trend over five decades* while reducing the error of missing cases as large events are much more likely to be covered by media outlets and offer the best information when making comparisons across countries and world regions (Koopmans, 1999; Hutter, 2014).

By focusing on neoliberal policy-related protest events throughout this study, we also ensure evidence that is based on resistance to market fundamentalism. This is an advantage over studies that connect neoliberal policies *to general social conflict of protests, riots, strikes, and violent uprisings* whereby the protest participants may or may not be directly making claims related to market reforms. These studies are most common when using preexisting conflict data sets that do not specify the goals or claims of the protest participants (e.g., the

Banks' Cross-National Time-Series Data Archive). Section 2 draws largely on the Large-Scale Anti-Neoliberal Protest Data Base and the subnational and transnational protest event data sets. Section 3 uses secondary sources and field research conducted by the authors. Section 4 explores the current phase of neoliberalism, alternative economic practices, and future warnings.

2 Temporal Rhythms and the Geography of Revolt

This section addresses the temporal and geographic variation of movements and campaigns challenging the deepening of neoliberal policymaking. The approach analyzes different scales of collective action from the local to the international – as resistance to the erosion of social citizenship rights appears as multiscalar (Kousis, 2016). We focus on the differences between the drivers of collective resistance in the global North and global South, with an emphasis on recessions versus structural adjustment programs. Attention is also given to the subnational variation in anti-neoliberal collective action. In other words, within countries, which regions and localities seem more likely to mobilize? We conclude the section with a discussion on the growth of transnational campaigns against neoliberalism.

Resistance Over Time, 1970 to the Present

The first stages of austerity in the global North unleashed a series of defensive strikes by public and industrial labor unions in the 1970s. Once states institutionalized austerity programs by the early 1980s, they became standard operating procedure to manage subsequent rounds of economic slowdowns. Table 2 documents some of the largest outbreaks of austerity protest in the global North in the late 1970s using the Large-Scale Anti-Neoliberal Protest Data Base. From Canada to Japan, protest campaigns and strikes erupted over price inflation and cutbacks to state budgets. Public sector unions (including municipal-level employees) and schoolteachers led the anti-austerity protests in North America. In Europe, labor confederations organized the largest strikes and demonstrations.

Even though the term "neoliberalism" did not become a common label for market fundamentalism until the late 1980s and 1990s, the policies of economic deregulation began in the 1970s. The transition in the 1970s is important to document for multiple reasons. One is to recognize the economic formations that came before neoliberalism in terms of more state-guided economies and an uneven expansion of social citizenship rights. Such acknowledgments contribute to contrasting neoliberalism with previous state-economic relationships and avoid essentializing or de-historicizing the concept. Second, once governments

Table 2 Major campaigns in global North against austerity, 1975–9

Date	Country	Description
1975	Spain	Protests, boycotts, and strikes in different cities (Valladolid, Madrid) against high prices, and for labor demands
1975	Greece	48-hour strikes mounted by public employees, for higher wages and payment of a week's salary
1975	Canada	Month-long strike at Vancouver and five other British Columbia ports brought dry cargo shipping on the West Coast to a complete halt (April). Strike was over job security. Nationwide postal strike (November/ December)
1975	Italy	Wave of strikes: About 300,000 civil servants and firemen struck May 6–7, shutting down government offices and halting traffic at Rome's international airport. Protests over wage demands
1975	USA	Demonstrations and strikes in different cities against layoffs, rising taxes, and slashing municipal services. United Mine Workers national strike. Teachers in twelve states were on strike by the first week of September
1975	France	Unions hold demonstrations throughout France protesting the government economic program (September)
1975	Japan	An estimated 860,000 Japanese public corporation and government workers walked off their jobs November 26, tying up the nation's transport and communication systems
1976	Spain	A series of strikes swept Spanish cities in October and November as workers demanded pay increases and protested a government austerity program
1977	France	A 24-hour nationwide strike of 150,000 postal workers against austerity plans (January). Millions of French workers participated in a 24-hour general strike against austerity plan (May)
1978	France	A large number of strikes and job actions against austerity were reported during June in many parts of France
1979	United Kingdom	Protests denounce Prime Minister Margaret Thatcher, and protests against the $3.5 billion cut in public spending, affecting schools, hospitals, transport and municipal services (November)

Source: Large-Scale Anti-Neoliberal Protest Data Base (created by the authors based on Nexis Uni, Global NewsBank, SCAD, and PRIO, 1970–79).

began to adjust to the global economic recession of the early 1970s and enact major austerity measures, civil society organizations mounted campaigns of resistance by the mid- to late 1970s. This early resistance to neoliberalism is often missing from social movement accounts of mobilization against free market reforms and economic liberalization (see Table 2). Finally, much of the organizational basis of the opposition to neoliberalism derives from the public and economic infrastructure established and expanded in the previous period of Keynesianism and state-led development.

Figure 3 highlights the rhythms of resistance in the global North and global South over the long term as indicated by large-scale collective campaigns against market fundamentalism. Oppositional groups in both parts of the globe initiated extensive collective action in the mid- to late 1970s in the aftermath of the 1973 economic recession. The onset of the Third World debt crisis drove a spike in large-scale campaigns in the global South in the mid-1980s. The push toward privatization of the public sector by IMF and World Bank structural adjustment policies sustained major protest campaigns in the global South in the late 1990s and 2000s. Indeed, Africa, followed by Latin America, experienced the greatest number of large-scale anti-neoliberal campaigns between 2000 and 2009 (more than any other world region). Europe once again displayed resistance with mass protests over austerity in the mid-1990s (especially in Germany) as governments slashed budgets to prepare for launching the unitary European currency. The Great Recession of 2008/2009 and the European Debt Crisis, propelled anti-austerity protests to new heights in Europe in the early 2010s (Della Porta, 2015; Kriesi, 2020; Bojar et al., 2021).

As noted in Section 1, several anti-neoliberal campaigns broke out in 2019 in the global South, including the multitudinous uprisings in Chile with street demonstrations reaching a million participants. Even with the downward trend of collective protests in the middle of the Covid pandemic and public health lockdowns between 2020 and 2022, massive outbreaks of economic-based protests occurred in India, Tunisia, Costa Rica, Colombia, Sri Lanka, Kazakhstan, Panama, and Ecuador – a clear sign that contention over market reforms continues into the third decade of the twenty-first century.

Figure 4 demonstrates that austerity measures act as the dominant economic policy motivating mass mobilization in the global North and South. In the global South, even though austerity acts as the central threat driving protest campaigns, there is a greater mix of additional neoliberal policies, including price hikes (associated with deregulation) and privatization. This pattern is consistent with Roberts's (2008) assertion that there are a variety of drivers of anti-neoliberal protest. These differences are largely due to the conditionality agreements most global South states must enact that often involve raising

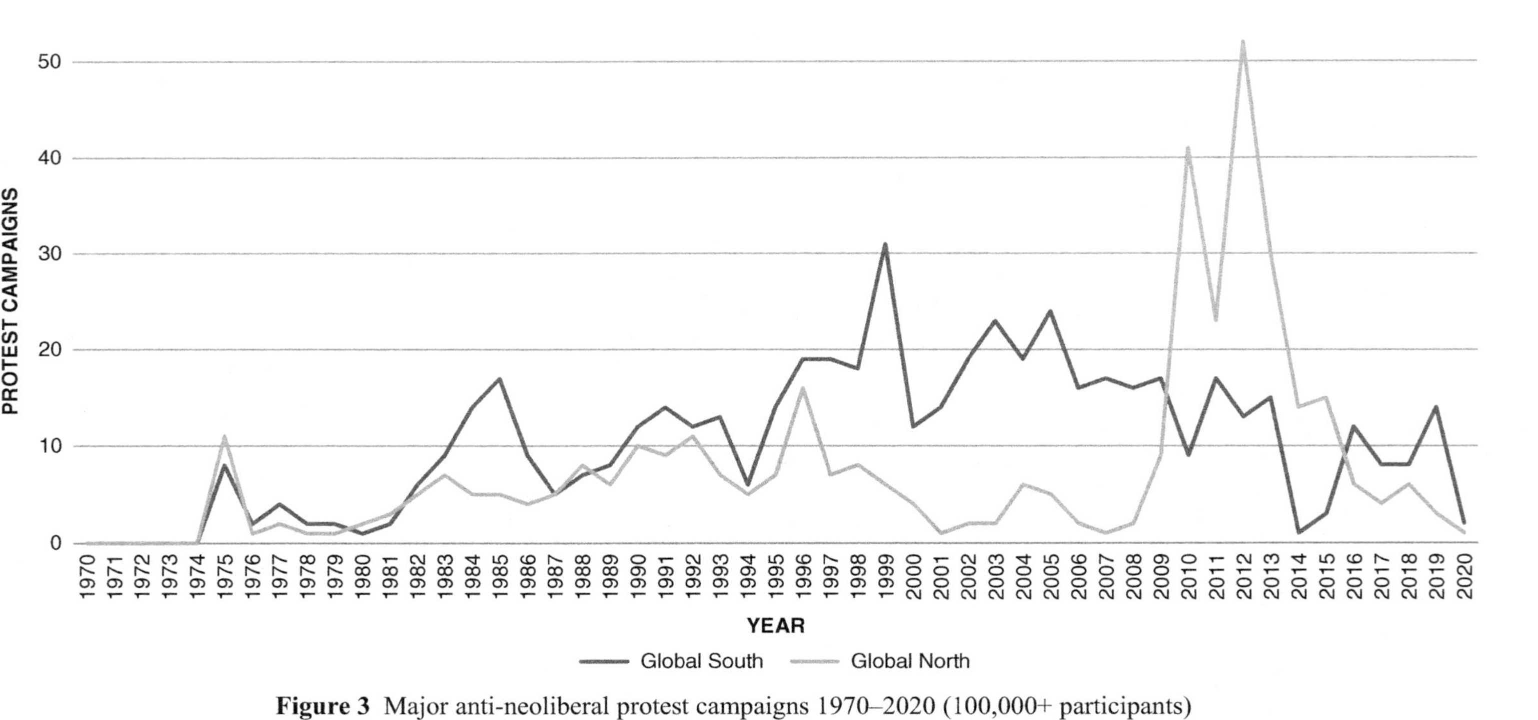

Figure 3 Major anti-neoliberal protest campaigns 1970–2020 (100,000+ participants)

Source: Large-Scale Anti-Neoliberal Protest Data Base (created by the authors based on Nexis Uni, Global NewsBank, SCAD, and PRIO, 1970–2020).

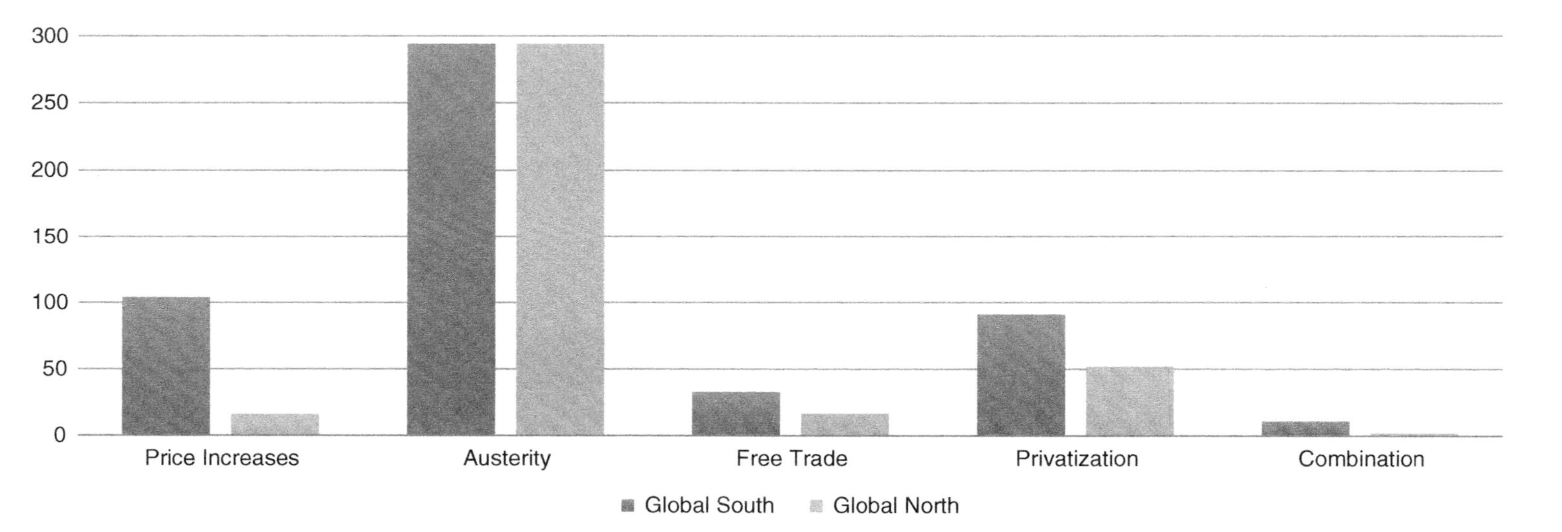

Figure 4 Drivers of major anti-neoliberal protest campaigns 1970–2020 (100,000+ participants)

Source: Large-Scale Anti-Neoliberal Protest Data Base (created by the authors based on Nexis Uni and Global NewsBank, SCAD, and PRIO, 1970–2020).

consumer prices and privatization in addition to standard austerity measures (see Figure 1). Privatization and free trade emerged as major threats in pushing collective action in the 1990s and 2000s in tandem with a deepening of neoliberalism on a global scale. Although intensive nation-based protest campaigns against free trade agreements emerged in the global South, there were several notable transnational mobilizations against the World Trade Organization (WTO), G8, and Free Trade Area of the Americas (FTAA) in the global North in the late 1990s and early 2000s.

The question of multiple social sectors in major episodes of contention against the erosion of social citizenship rights is introduced in Figure 5. In all world regions, with the exception of Latin America, campaigns were dominated more often by one leading sector. In Africa and Asia, only about 36 percent of major protest campaigns against neoliberalism involved multiple sectors. In most cases, the primary sector was some form of labor organization, such as a public sector labor federation, a national teachers' union, or a general confederation of labor unions. In the global North, there is more of a balance with 46 percent of major campaigns involving multiple sectors in the protest. In Latin America, 55 percent of large-scale campaigns incorporated multiple sectors. The Latin American exception may be due to the development of social

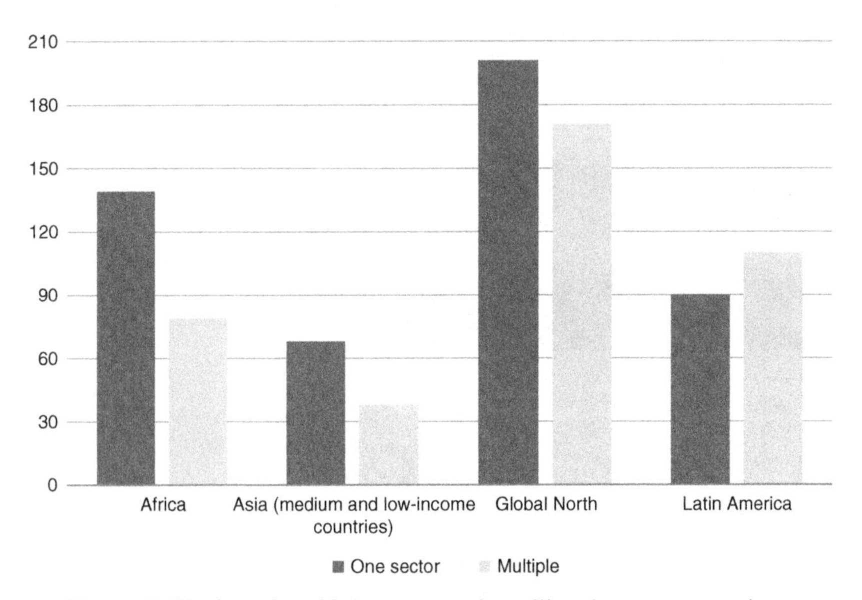

Figure 5 Single and multiple sector anti-neoliberal protest campaigns, 1970–2020

Source: Large-Scale Anti-Neoliberal Protest Data Base (created by the authors from Nexis Uni and Global NewsBank, SCAD, and PRIO, 1970–2020).

movement unionism in countries such as Brazil and Argentina, whereby unions seek to build alliances with community organizations and other movements outside of the labor sector. Section 3 explores the question of coalitions in more detail in a variety of anti-neoliberal campaigns in terms of outcomes.

Economic Recessions and Resistance in the Global North

The general pattern for mobilized opposition to neoliberalism in the global North appears synchronized with major economic recessions, especially the recessions of the early 1970s, early 1980s, early 1990s, and the Great Recession of 2008/2009 (see Tables 2 and 3 and Figure 3). The long recession, OPEC oil crisis, and stagflation of the 1970s marked the end of the post-Second World War economic boom and the initial stages of the implementation of substantial state cutbacks. Large protest campaigns against neoliberalism in the global North continued to occur into the early 1980s during the second major postwar recession (see Table 3). At this time, workers, civil servants, and consumers largely reacted to the erosion of social benefits, weakening of collective bargaining contracts, and the rising cost of living. Deep into the decade of the 1980s the term "Neoliberalism" was still just an economic philosophy largely restricted to academic discussion that had not trickled down to mainstream discourse.

The Large-Scale Anti-Neoliberal Protest Data Base used in Tables 2 and 3 (and Figure 3) involved either a minimum of 100,000 protest participants and/or occurred on a nationwide level. Hence, we established a relatively precise timeline for both the onset of neoliberalism and the first series of major mobilizations by civil society to turn back the undesirable changes in the global North. In these first decades of resistance to neoliberalism there is a heavy presence of labor unions and state sector employees. By the 1990s and 2000s, the coalition diversified into more representation from other social sectors and groups.

The Great Recession of 2008/2009 unleashed an even greater round of anti-austerity protest in the global North (see Figure 3). Just as with the global recessions of 1973–5, 1980–83, and 1990–91, there was a lag effect for the full policy consequences to be implemented across North America and continental Europe in the early 2010s. Both the Lehman Brothers shock of 2008[3] and the larger Eurozone crisis of 2010 gave impetus to a variety of nation-based austerity programs and protest campaigns in the global North (Kriesi, 2020). These include the "pot and pans" protests in Iceland (Bernburg, 2015), the

[3] The Lehman Brothers shock refers to the economic crisis resulting from the filing for bankruptcy of the Lehman Brothers global financial firm in September 2008 related to subprime mortgage loans, unpaid debt, and falling real estate prices. The failure of Lehman Brothers precipitated the larger global recession enduring into 2009.

Table 3 Major episodes and campaigns in global North against austerity, 1980–83

Date	Country	Description
1980	Poland	120,000 Polish workers strike as meat price increases. Strike spreads to 174 factories in multiple cities (August)
1980	Italy	9 million Italian workers stage a nationwide general strike over unemployment insurance, and mass layoffs (October)
1981	Belgium	Demonstrations against government austerity program, which is expected to freeze income of citizens (January)
1981	Poland	100,000 (strike), 5,000 (protest), more than 1 million workers (walkout) in a wave of food protests. Rallies held in six cities over mounting food shortages and price increases (August)
1981	Italy	10 million Italians participate in four-hour national strike against austerity programs meant to limit pay increases (October)
1982	Italy	Crowds of more than 10 million Italian workers rallied in Rome and millions of others stopped work in a general strike against government austerity plans to stop cost of living wage increases. Workers participated in an eight-hour protest that shut down industries, banks, schools, postal services, and garbage collection (June)
1982	Germany	380,000 people took to the streets to voice grievances against unemployment and welfare cuts (October). 100,000 demonstrate in Hamburg and Saarbrücken to protest against unemployment and government cuts to welfare expenditure (November)
1982	Denmark	In Copenhagen, 150,000 demonstrate with multiple protests against government austerity that would eliminate cost of living raises and impose wage freezes (October)
1982	France	In Paris, workers strike to protest the governments planned wage restraints (October)
1983	Italy	4-hour general strike to protest government austerity measures that call for scaling down the nation's automatic cost of living wage increase agreements and reducing public spending in health care and pension benefits. Largest crowds reported in Rome (100,000), Florence (50,000 people marched), Turin, Bologna, Naples, and Genoa against austerity program (January)

Table 3 (cont.)

Date	Country	Description
1983	Belgium	Brussels, 500,000 in demonstration demanding the government create more jobs using money saved through its austerity measures (February)
1983	Japan	Hundreds of thousands of labor union members, shouting "down with unfair taxation," demonstrated at 23 rallies across Japan to demand reform of regressive taxes (March)
1983	Ireland	100,000 workers marched in Dublin and other cities to protest increases in taxes and social security contributions. Demonstrations in 19 other cities, demonstrators called for efforts to provide more jobs as well as tax reductions (April)
1983	Germany	130,000 steel and shipworkers protest in West Germany against unemployment and the economic policies of the conservative Government of Chancellor Helmut Kohl. Rally at Bonn University (September)
1983	Belgium	900,000 civil servants across Belgium on strike to protest government austerity plan. It is a wildcat walkout with 25 percent of public-school teachers and employees on strike and a two-week strike by Belgium's public workers (September)
1983	Portugal	In Lisbon, 100,000 demonstrate while rallies are held in 21 cities across the country against increases in taxes and prices and against the privatization of state enterprises (October)
1983	Canada	100,000 workers in schools and government offices on strike to save jobs. Government plans to cut the civil service by 25 percent and more than 250,000 workers (November)

Source: Large-Scale Anti-Neoliberal Protest Data Base (created by the authors from Nexis Uni, Global NewsBank, SCAD, and PRIO, 1980–83).

Indignados mobilizations in Spain, the Occupy Wall Street movement in the United States, and the massive civil society resistance to austerity in Greece and Portugal, among many other cases. In an analysis of nearly 30,000 protest events of all types across continental Europe between 2000 and 2015, Gessler and Schulte-Cloos (2020) found that that the largest percentage by far of collective actions (26 percent) focused on *economic demands* directed toward the government.

Structural Adjustment and Resistance in the Global South

While resistance to neoliberalism proliferated in the global North in the mid- to late 1970s, there were a few major outbreaks in the global South, including in Bolivia, Colombia, Jamaica, Egypt, Chile, and Peru (as observed in Figure 3). For example, in Colombia in September 1977, civic organizations coordinated a national civic strike (*el paro cívico nacional*) against the high cost of living. An estimated 1.3 million people participated in the strike (more than 1 in 25 Colombians) (Medina, 1999). But the major driver of resistance centered on the Third World debt crisis beginning in the early 1980s (Walton and Seddon, 1994). The debt crisis occurred over the drastic changes in the interest rates on previous foreign loans and the falling commodity prices for global South primary exports. Very few loans were negotiated between international financial institutions and countries in the global South between the 1950s and 1970s and interest rates remained relatively stable. These conditions shifted markedly with the onset of the balance of payments crisis in the early 1980s throughout the global South. As stated in Section 1, the IMF and World Bank stepped in to manage the Third World debt crisis in the 1980s, beginning with Mexico's temporary default on payments in 1982. Several large-N cross-national studies now indicate that structural adjustment programs resulted in negative outcomes in terms of the quality of life (Abouharb et al., 2015), health (Kentikelenis, 2017), and human rights (Abouharb and Cingranelli, 2007) in countries undergoing long-term conditionality.

Structural adjustment borrowing also expanded to Eastern Europe and nations in the former Soviet Union in the 1990s. The IMF received a new infusion of investment from G20 countries in 2009 in the midst of the Great Recession (Kentikelenis et al., 2016). With this expansion in geographical reach and financing, the IMF and World Bank continued conditionality lending into the 2010s and 2020s (see Figure 1). Indeed, the massive anti-IMF uprising by indigenous populations and popular sectors in Ecuador between 2019 and 2022, and the rural anti-IMF protests in Costa Rica in 2020 (discussed later) demonstrate the ongoing contested nature of structural adjustment in the contemporary era (Ortiz Crespo, 2020). While not all resistance to neoliberalism in the global South is directly related to structural adjustment programs, many large-scale campaigns are at least indirectly related to conditionality agreements or the institutionalization of neoliberal practices as standard operating procedure. The specific conditionality policies most commonly inducing defensive collective action include austerity measures, price increases, privatization, free trade, and labor sector flexibility.

Resistance Across Territories

Most work on resistance to anti-neoliberal policy implementation is carried out in single case studies, often at the national and transnational levels. We know much less about the variation in resistance to market reforms across geographic regions *within* countries. In the global North, analysts compare anti-neoliberal protests across cities, counties, and provinces. In the global South, campaigns of sustained action often emerge from activist-created structures such as labor unions, cooperatives, indigenous people's associations, and popular organizations. Campaigns also originate from everyday organizations such as religious institutions, schools, and NGOs. Likewise, the presence of state infrastructures increases the likelihood of collective action involving administrative offices, highways (creating occasions to disrupt economic activities), and large development projects that intensify resource extraction and extend the capacity for international trade and investment (e.g., China's Belt and Road Initiative in more than seventy countries). Blocking major transportation routes and highways has served as one of the preferred repertoires of contention in the global South. For example, in the October 2019 indigenous and popular uprising against the IMF in Ecuador, a reported 392 roadblocks occurred on the major highways and another 1,228 barricades occurred on other urban streets and rural roads across the country (Ortiz Crespo, 2020). Increasingly, in the global South the use of social media platforms provides a tremendous jump in scale for collective action, especially WhatsApp, Telegram, Twitter, Facebook, Instagram and other direct messaging services on cellphones (Tufekci, 2017). The tremendous growth in the past two decades of ICT infrastructure in the global South and mass accessibility are documented in Section 1.

Subnational Resistance in the Global North

In the global North, subnational resistance to neoliberalism has largely been analyzed through major campaigns such as Occupy Wall Street (OWS) in the United States and the long-term struggles of the labor movement. Gillham et al. (2019) find that economic threats (in the form of high-income inequality) explained mobilization at the county level in the OWS movement in the fall of 2011 along with the density of labor and civic organizations. In a city-level analysis of the United States, Vasi and Suh (2016) demonstrated that occupy encampments were associated with universities, past progressive activism, and preexisting local social media sites supporting the OWS campaign. In a study of OWS across California cities, Curran et al. (2015) found a positive association of city-level OWS Facebook pages with university density and electoral support for the Democratic Party.

In the labor sector, Martin and Dixon (2010) demonstrate that resistance to the transition from Fordism to neoliberalism through strike activity in the United States was most common in states with high labor union membership and a higher number of labor unions. In another subnational study of the US labor movement from 1947 to 2003, Abouharb and Fordham (2020) show that economic threat created by the uncertainty of international trade increases state-level strikes in the short term. They also find worker resistance to the transition to neoliberalism in the form of strikes is more common in states with higher levels of union density and past strike activity. Almeida (2019b), in a county-level analysis of Fight for $15 fast food worker strikes for a livable wage between 2013 and 2017, suggests that resistance is linked to proximity of SEIU labor union organizing efforts (Padilla, in press).

Between 2007 and 2012, Palmtag et al. (2020) examined protests against international trade across seventy-five regions in Russia and found the highest counts of popular contention occurring in localities experiencing an elevated backlash of economic grievances from globalization – a form of economic threat. During the financial crisis in Greece between 2010 and 2012, in each of the thirty-two large protest episodes occurring in Athens against austerity, Kousis states,

> the protest campaign was also carried out across a majority of Greek towns and cities. Thus the 32 major events, most of which ended in demonstrations facing the Greek Parliament in Athens' Syntagma Square, were accompanied by a total number of 1,069 parallel protest events across the country, all with the same repertoire of claims (Kousis, 2016: 163).

By 2014, more than 20,000 protest events were reported in Greece. Facebook played a large part in mobilizing thirty-eight cities in Greece in the early phases of the anti-austerity campaigns in 2010 (especially encampments in town squares), along with left parties, labor unions, and students and parents (Kousis, 2016). In sum, subnational resistance in the global North to neoliberalism is most commonly found in those regions experiencing intensified economic threats and with a variety of resource infrastructures – from civic organizations/labor unions and digital networking to strategic experience in past collective action.

Subnational Resistance in the Global South

While resistance to free market fundamentalism often occurs with the greatest intensity in capital cities in the global South, many protest campaigns encompass large parts of the national territory. Latin America alone has witnessed hundreds of protest campaigns against some type of neoliberal policy whereby opponents coordinated collective action in multiple towns, villages, and transportation routes outside of the principal cities. Such nationwide campaigns go back to the late 1970s in Peru against the austerity of the Morales-Bermúdez military regime (Roberts, 1998), as well as campaigns in Jamaica, Colombia, and Bolivia. In the 1980s, major nationwide campaigns took place in Mexico against austerity (in 1983), in Costa Rica against IMF-mandated electricity price hikes (in 1983), and against an IMF austerity package in Panama (Beluche, 1994). Also, in the early 1980s, Argentina, Bolivia, Brazil, Dominican Republic, Jamaica, Ecuador, Panama, Peru, and Uruguay experienced nationally coordinated protest campaigns against austerity with events scattered across their national territories.

One exemplary case from the early 1980s involved anti-austerity mobilization in Mexico. Mexico was one of the first countries to default on its foreign debt in 1982 after years of heavy borrowing (to fund state and industrial infrastructure expansion) and then a collapse in international petroleum prices. To manage the debt crisis the PRI government of Miguel de la Madrid immediately enacted austerity policies – i.e., el Programa Inmediato de Reordenación Económica (PIRE) – in a decisive shift from state-led development and import substitution industrialization (ISI) (Haber, 2006). In response, an unprecedented coalition of civil society forces formed in late 1982 into two coordinating umbrella organizations: El Frente Nacional en Defensa del Salario, Contra la Austeridad y la Carestía (FNDSCAC) and El Comité de Defensa de la Economía Popular (CNDEP). These two umbrella organizations included hundreds of urban popular organizations, student associations, and labor unions. Throughout the first half of 1983, FNDSCAC and CNDEP solidified their respective coalitions to challenge the austerity package and in June unified in the Asamblea Nacional Obrera, Campesina, y Popular (ANOCP) (Cadena-Roa, 1988). The high point of these mobilizing efforts occurred on October 18, 1983 when the multisectoral ANOCP coalition held a national civic strike with an estimated 1.5 million participants (UPI, 1983). A reported 500 actions took place in 150 localities (López Pardo, 1984), including a march of 10,000 in the city of Oaxaca and several protests organized by community-based organizations (CBOs) and labor unions. Figure 6 shows the subnational distribution of participation in the 1983 anti-austerity strike. Another attempt at a second national strike was held in June of 1984, but was much weaker. In the aftermath of the second civic strike, the coalitions began to loosen and eventually disintegrate.

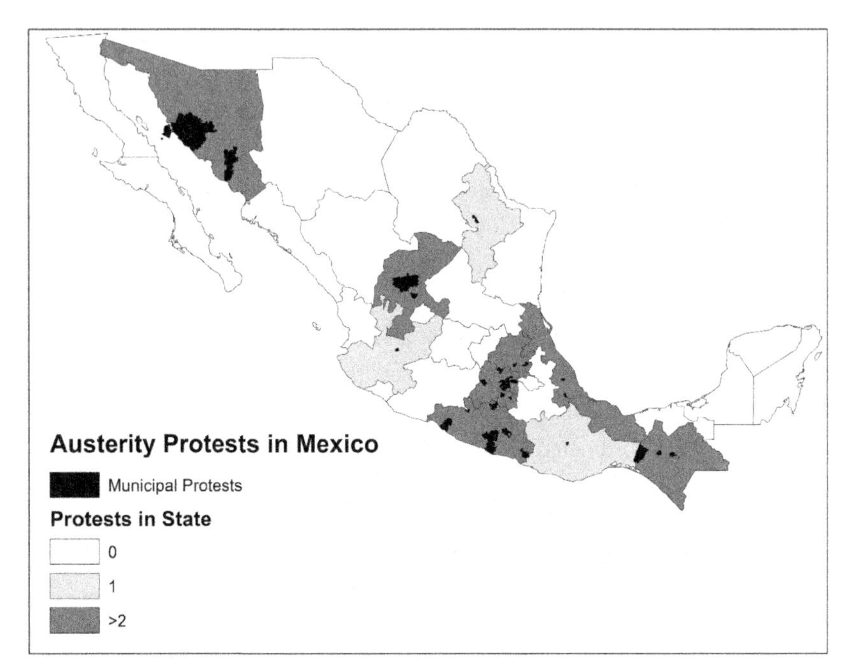

Figure 6 National civic strike participation in Mexico in October 1983
Source: Created by the authors from Barbosa Cano and González Arévalo (1984).

Mexico is the second largest country in Latin America and the failure to turn back the initiation of free market reforms via a mobilized opposition portended similar outcomes throughout the global South – mass mobilization confronting the ongoing deepening of neoliberalism. The social consequences of the economic reforms throughout the 1980s in Mexico were startling. The number of people living in poverty grew from 18.4 million citizens in 1981 to 41.3 million in 1988, along with severe cuts in public and social spending (Haber, 2006: 60).

Elsewhere in Latin America from 1985 to 1989, massive multi-city actions against economic adjustments took place in Brazil, Argentina, El Salvador, Haiti, Peru, and Trinidad. Other regions of the global South also experienced widespread protests across their national territories in the 1980s in response to structural adjustment and economic liberalization. These cases include the Philippines, Israel, Tunisia, India, Morocco, Sierra Leone, South Africa, Sudan, Zambia, Bangladesh, Nigeria, Algeria, and Jordan.[4] The diversity and frequency of large-scale anti-neoliberal actions increased in the 1990s and

[4] These cases come from data introduced by authors in Section 1 of protest campaigns larger than 100,000 participants or occurring in multiple cities.

2000s with greater intensity in the interior provinces throughout the global South (see Figure 3).

By the 2010s and early 2020s, additional massive campaigns with hundreds of events scattered across national territories continued, with particularly spectacular episodes against economic cutbacks in Iran (2017/2018 and 2019), Chile (2019), Colombia (2013, 2019, and 2021), Ecuador (2019, 2021 and 2022), Cuba (2021), and Kazakhstan (2022). The 2017/2018 "Dey" protest campaign in Iran included actions in up to 100 cities and towns over ten days against food prices, economic hardship, and unemployment. The campaign ended with twenty protesters killed and 4,000 arrested. The 2019 protest campaign (the Âbân protests) in Iran over a tripling of fuel prices occurred in 20 percent of the nation's counties with an empowered youth population contesting the erosion of long-term commitments to the welfare state (Kadivar et al., 2019). Severe repression followed the 2019 protests with up to 1,500 killed, 2,000 wounded, and 7,000 arrested as the state also shut down the Internet. The protest campaigns registered as the largest outbreaks of unrest since the 1979 Islamic Revolution, with the exception of the Green movement in 2009. Colombia also witnessed colossal protest campaigns with several hundred events in the cities and countryside between 2013 and 2021 over free trade, regressive taxation, educational fees, and health care privatization (Archila, 2021).[5] In Cuba, unprecedented massive anti-government protests erupted in impoverished territories across the country on July 11, 2021 to oppose both the lack of political freedoms and an unpopular new attempt at economic adjustment that aggravated the acute economic crisis in this country (Pérez Martín, in press).

The empirical studies of subnational protest against neoliberalism in the global South find similar correlates of protest intensity as reported in the global North in terms of the role of economic threats and prevailing resource infrastructures (Almeida, 2012). In a study of the unemployed workers' movement in neoliberal Argentina (*los piqueteros*), Arce and Mangonnet (2013) show anti-neoliberal protests and roadblocks driven by oppositional political parties, past protests in the region, and the economic threat of high unemployment levels. In Auyero and Moran's (2007) analysis of food riots in Argentina during the December 2001 national uprising against neoliberalism (*el Argentinazo*), they observed local variation in rioting based on the presence of Peronist party brokers.

In an extensive study of municipal-level collective action, Trejo (2012) examines 883 indigenous municipalities in Mexico over twenty-six years (1975–2000). The strongest predictors of indigenous people's protests include

[5] These major protest campaigns in Colombia include the August 2013 Paro Agrario, the November 2019 protests, and the April–May 2021 Paro Cívico protests.

neoliberal policy shifts in international trade (e.g., economic threat), local organization networks tied to the Catholic Church, and prior community experience with social movement mobilization. The Zapatista rebellion in southern Mexico that began in 1994 also offers another emblematic case of subnational resistance to neoliberalism (as a response to the North American Free Trade Agreement). Inclán's (2018) local-level study of the Zapatista rebellion in the state of Chiapas across 111 municipalities between 1994 and 2003, finds that municipalities with past protest experience recorded higher rates of protest. In early 2017, another major national campaign broke out in Mexico over the deregulation of PEMEX and the rise in fuel prices. More than a thousand protest events were reported, and demonstrations took place in twenty-nine out of thirty-one provincial capital cities. Demonstrators employed the roadblock as a dominant part of their repertoire of resistance with 71 percent of municipalities documenting a protest also intersected by a major highway (Almeida, 2019b).

In both the global South and the global North, past protest experience is a consistent predictor of resistance to neoliberalism at the subnational level. While several studies demonstrate past protest experience in general correlates with anti-neoliberal protest, we would expect *previous collective action around market reforms* to be an especially powerful predictor of the geographical distribution of protest events against neoliberalism (Flesher Fominaya, 2017). Major anti-neoliberal protest campaigns in the past infuse communities with collective efficacy, organizing skills, and frames of interpreting free market policy implementation. The organizational and ideational resources remain in communities long after the campaign ends and can be drawn upon by local activists and leaders in the future in the next round of structural adjustment or economic liberalization (Almeida, 2014; Almeida et al., 2021).

Subnational Case Study of Costa Rica

In order to observe the subnational components in resisting neoliberalism at the local level, we provide a fine-grained analysis of Costa Rica. Costa Rica has undergone several rounds of structural adjustment and free market reforms since the early 1980s. It has historically served as an exemplar of the "tropical welfare state" in the era of state-led development with the establishment of nearly one hundred new state institutions between 1950 and 1980 (Edelman, 1999). The Costa Rican state provides one of the most extensive health care systems in the global South with universal coverage. The country also has an expansive education system, including in higher education. It maintains an elaborate state infrastructure of utilities, social services, and community development programs designed explicitly to protect low-income and vulnerable populations. Despite these gains, Costa Rica's internal budget deficits and external debt have placed the country under pressure to cut back in welfare state investments and to privatize its public infrastructure over the past several decades. These conditions of sizable social citizenship benefits with ongoing threats to weaken them, make Costa Rica a social laboratory to understand local-level resistance to neoliberalism.

After several major battles over austerity and structural adjustment led by consumers, rural producers, teachers, and state workers in the 1980s and 1990s, an even more intensive conflict erupted in early 2000 over the privatization of Costa Rica's electricity and telecommunication systems – the Instituto de Comunicaciones y Electricidad (ICE). The ICE stood out as a high mark for state-led development in Costa Rica (Haglund, 2010). The Costa Rican government first established the ICE in 1949. By 1980, nearly 80 percent of households were connected to electrical power. By the late 1980s, Costa Ricans had phone access nearly three times the Latin American average. When the Costa Rican parliament passed legislation seeking to privatize the ICE in March of 2000, the resistance from civil society was swift and massive. Raventós (2018) states that the protests against the privatization were the largest in decades and the coalitions that formed the opposition proved decisive in the subsequent struggle against the Central American Free Trade Agreement (CAFTA). In March and early April 2000, a reported 473 protest events occurred across the national territory. More than half of the events were roadblocks. The anti-privatization campaign was successful and prevented the privatization.

For this study we are primarily concerned with explaining two other (and even larger) mobilizations against neoliberalism at the subnational level in Costa Rica: the campaign against the Central American Free Trade Agreement (CAFTA) from 2003 to 2007 and the campaign against a new IMF agreement in 2020. The protest campaign against CAFTA in Costa Rica stood out as the largest in Central America. The Free Trade Agreement threatened multiple components of Costa Rica's tropical welfare state, including telecommunications, the health care system (in terms of the pricing of pharmaceuticals), and the environment in terms of mining, and intellectual property rights of seeds, plants, and other natural resources. The CAFTA campaign produced a reported 694 protest events, including several general strikes and two mass marches of 200,000 participants. Figure 7 illustrates the geographic distribution of the CAFTA protests in relation to the previous anti-privatization campaign. More than two-thirds of cantons (68 percent) that mobilized against the privatization of telecommunications and electricity in 2000 also held at least one protest event against CAFTA in the following years.

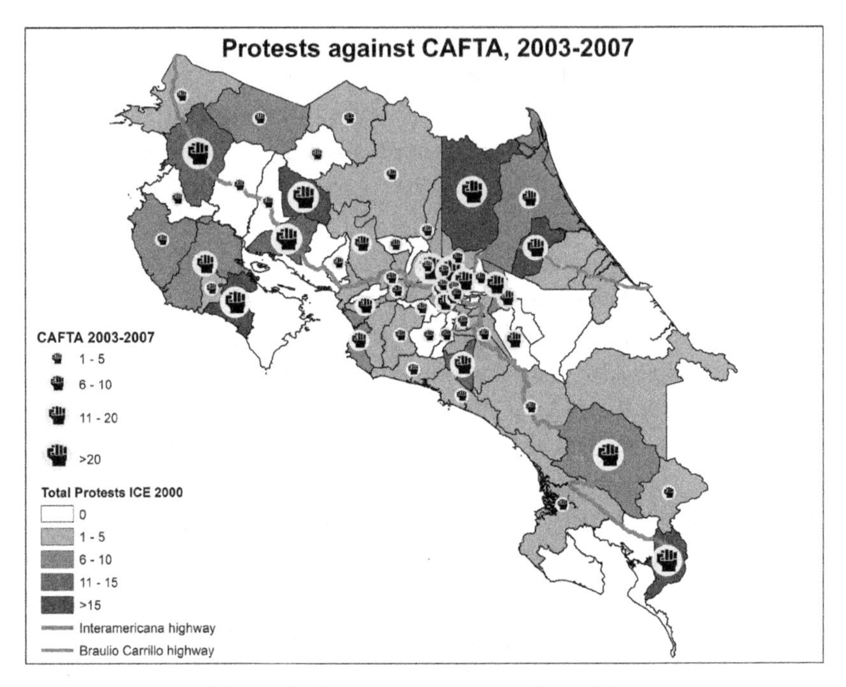

Figure 7 Free trade protest in Costa Rica
Source: Created by the authors from La Nación, Diario Extra, OSAL, Comisión Nacional de Enlace, La Prensa Libre, Seminario Universidad, La República.

Table 4 provides a multivariate count regression model examining the structural forces influencing anti-neoliberal protest at the local level against the Central American Free Trade Agreement in Costa Rica between 2003 and 2007. The table shows that the previous protests against privatization of the ICE were associated with increased counts of protest against CAFTA. In addition, highways and universities were also associated with heightened levels of protests at the local level. On some national days of protest, such as in August 2004, the highway blockade was a central tactic of the movement, as it is elsewhere in Latin America (Silva, 2009). Universities emerged early as a leading force of opposition against CAFTA. Eugenio Trejos Benavides, the rector of a Costa Rican University, even served as the president of one of the largest coalitions against the TLC – *El Movimiento Patriótico NO al TLC*. Universities led numerous protests, teach-ins, workshops, as well as publishing working papers on the dangers of CAFTA for Costa Rica.

In October of 2007, on the heels of a massive demonstration of 200,000 people to close out the "No on CAFTA" campaign, the opposition to CAFTA suffered a narrow defeat as the country voted in a national referendum 51.6 percent to 48.4 percent to approve the free trade treaty. Nonetheless, the mobilizations were

Table 4 Negative binomial count regression predicting protests against CAFTA

Independent Variables	**Model 1**
Protests against Privatization	.010*
	(.007)
Public Universities	.914**
	(.379)
Highway	.619*
	(.315)
Provincial Capital	.406
	(.281)
Population (ln)	.812***
	(.087)
Log psuedolikelihood	-184.611
Pseudo R^2	.20
N	81

*p≤.05 **p≤.01 ***p≤.001 (one-tailed tests)
Note: Robust standard errors (clustered by province) in parentheses.

the largest in Central America against CAFTA, and the campaign demonstrated the critical role of past protest experience against neoliberalism (in the previous anti-privatization struggle), and the importance of everyday organizations and structures in facilitating mobilizations such as universities and highways that were established in the period of state-led development.

After the CAFTA defeat in the national referendum protests settled down, apart from a few smaller protest campaigns over mining and highway privatization in the 2010s. In 2018 another major campaign took off over fiscal reform. The fiscal reform protests were the third major campaign against neoliberalism in Costa Rica following the ICE privatization and CAFTA campaigns (Cordero et al., 2020). The protests lasted for ninety days between September and December 2018. More than 500 protests were recorded that included strikes, roadblocks, and street marches (Alvarado Alcázar and Martínez Sánchez, 2018). The fiscal reform centered on a regressive tax policy that targeted middle- and low-income earners to make up for the national government's fiscal deficit (Cordero, in press). One protest march on September 26, 2018, involved an estimated 500,000 participants, the largest street demonstration in Costa Rican history.

The campaign eventually failed as the fiscal reform tax law was approved by the legislature and courts in December 2018. The campaign revived social movement struggle on a national scale that had been dormant for a decade since the anti-CAFTA resistance ended in 2007. Observers noted the geographic reach of the 2018 fiscal reform campaign, with organizers mobilizing distant communities in the provinces of Limón, Puntarenas, and Guanacaste, whereby highway blockades were held along with popular assemblies (Cordero, in press).

The 2018 anti-neoliberal protest campaign set the stage for the 2020 anti-IMF protests. The Covid pandemic immediately doubled unemployment and placed 30 percent of the population in poverty, the highest level in three decades (Alvarado Alcázar et al., 2020). In the first year of the pandemic, in August 2020, the Costa Rican government signed a loan agreement with the IMF and began negotiating a second loan of $1.75 billion in September. The second loan negotiations triggered a massive protest campaign between late September and October 2020 with roadblocks occurring across the national territory (Alvarado Alcázar et al., 2020). Between late September and October, there were 618 anti-IMF protest events documented. They were largely roadblocks and non-institutional actions (Alvarado Alcázar et al., 2020). The overwhelming outpouring of popular dissent forced the government to temporarily pause the second loan negotiations with the IMF and enter into dialogue with the sectors in opposition. Nonetheless, the government went ahead and signed the $1.75 billion loan with the IMF in March 2021. Figure 8 maps the protests against the IMF agreement in 2020 with the Fiscal Reform protests in 2018.

Table 5 provides a multivariate count regression model examining the structural forces influencing anti-neoliberal protest at the local level against the 2020 IMF loan in Costa Rica. The results are similar to the protests against CAFTA. The recent strategic experience of protesting against the fiscal tax reform was associated with increased local resistance against the 2020 IMF agreement. Especially effective was the 2018 campaign's ability to reach rural populations that had not been mobilized for at least a decade. Indeed, 77 percent of localities mobilizing against the 2018 neoliberal regressive tax plan also mobilized two years later against the IMF. Highways were a key component of the 2020 anti-IMF campaign as strategic sites to construct barricades and obstruct transportation and commerce to leverage the central government into negotiations. The negative impact of provincial capitals on the rate of protest demonstrates the rural nature of the resistance to the IMF.

Transnational Resistance against Neoliberalism

Several precursors to the anti-neoliberal transnational movements of the twenty-first century occurred in past centuries. Perhaps the most prominent

Table 5 Negative binomial count regression predicting protests against IMF in 2020

Independent Variables	**Model 1**
Protests against Fiscal Reform 2018	.166***
	(.049)
Public Universities	.908*
	(.448)
Highway	.496*
	(.248)
Provincial Capital	-2.454***
	(.431)
Population (ln)	.052
	(.282)
Log psuedolikelihood	-214.326
Pseudo R^2	.08
N	81

*p≤.05 **p≤.01 ***p≤.001 (two-tailed tests)

Note: Robust standard errors (clustered by province) in parentheses.

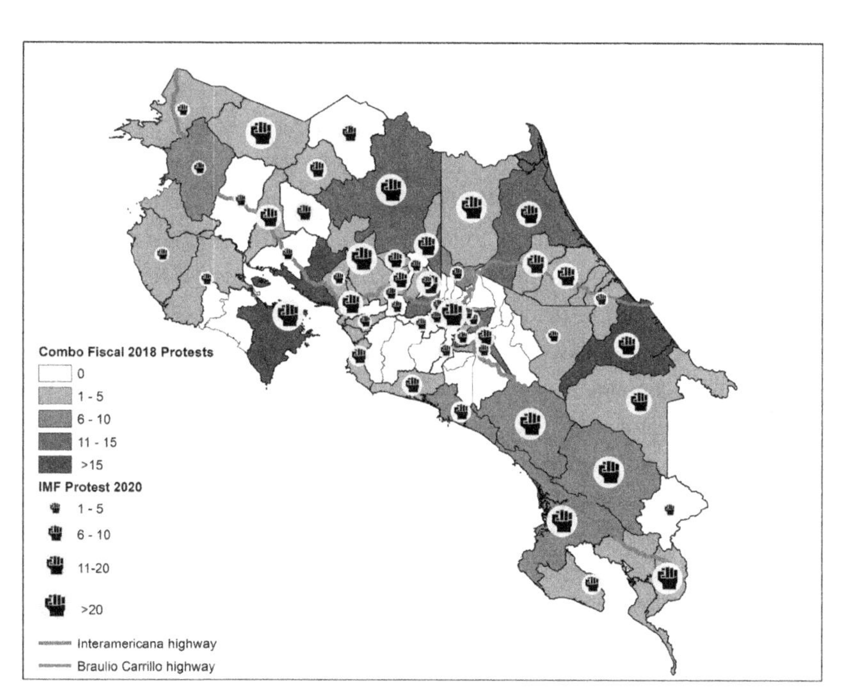

Figure 8 IMF protests in Costa Rica, 2020

Source: Created by the authors based on Alvarado Alcázar and Martínez Sánchez (2021).

initiatives include the multiple labor and socialist internationals and the Cuban-initiated Tricontinental movement in the global South in the 1960s and 1970s (Wood, 2012; Garland Mahler, 2018). Nation states in the world system played a larger role in these earlier international alliances than the current grassroots-based transnational movements confronting economic globalization such as Via Campesina. Other more recent developments also contributed to constructing a template and international networks for the rise of transnational movements against neoliberalism, including United Nations conferences focusing on women, the environment, and development and alternative counter-meetings to the annual summit of the G7 countries. Between the 1970s and 1990s, these forerunner transnational events often involved civil society groups and nongovernmental organizations (Pianta and Marchetti, 2007).

The takeoff point for transnational resistance to neoliberalism began in the mid-1990s with international solidarity for the anti-free trade and indigenous Zapatista movement in Mexico (Andrews, 2010) and the initial mobilizations against the World Trade Organization (WTO) and other international financial bodies (Lichbach, 2003). At the dawn of the twenty-first century, the innovation in internet communication technologies (ICTs) also surfaced just as the global economic justice movement gained momentum. Activist-based internet websites in multiple languages served to coordinate actions on an international scale (e.g., Independent Media, Peoples Global Action, and ATTAC), while cellphones and email assisted in the assembly of local actions, especially in the global North. There was a cooling effect in the global economic justice movement after the September 11, 2001 attacks and the war on terrorism curtailed civil liberties throughout the global North, but especially in the United States and Canada (Hadden and Tarrow, 2007; Wood, 2012). The period from 2000 to 2002 served as the high point for the global economic justice movement, in terms of holding massive demonstrations combined with days of action around the globe (Flesher Fominaya, 2020a; Smith, 2020).

The global economic justice movement made several contributions to the international resistance to neoliberalism. The template of holding a focal event outside of an economic summit combined with simultaneous solidarity events in dozens of cities nationally and internationally increased mutual awareness about the negative impacts of free trade and the third world debt across the globe (Almeida and Lichbach, 2003). This template would be used by other related movements, including anti-war and climate justice in the years immediately after the peak of global economic justice street mobilizations in the early 2000s. The global economic justice movement, along with the growth of international nongovernmental organizations, provided an international infrastructure to contest neoliberalism on a planetary scale (Smith, 2008; Smith and Wiest, 2012). The use of the new ICT technologies and the cross-border relationships established the capacity to sustain mobilization into the 2010s, including the transnational peasant movement Via Campesina achieving the 2018 United Nations Declaration on the Rights of Peasants (Claeys and Edelman, 2020). Finally, the movement set the stage for the World Social Forum (WSF) process, a very positive self-correction of the global economic justice movement by moving the center of economic justice discussions to the global South and marginalized populations in the global North (in contrast to "summit hopping" of previous mobilizations).

Table 6 provides data on the largest global days of action against neoliberalism between 1999 and 2011. In the early 2000s, nations in the global North dominated in the transnational global justice movement in terms of their relative participation in campaigns against international financial institutions. The global South only contributed between 13 and 25 percent of the protest events during the height of the movement. However, with the call to action in the middle of the wave of protests against austerity and economic inequality in Europe and North America in late 2011, the participation by cities in the global South increased in absolute terms and in relative terms if we consider Spain and the United States as the "host countries" for the international day of action. Both Spain and the United States served as the models for the popular meetings and protests that were called to assemble on October 15, 2011.[6] Figure 9 maps the world geographic distribution of the 2011 events.

The increase in participation of the global South, even in campaigns largely organized by anti-austerity movements in the global North, acts as a positive trend toward developing a coordinated global response to market fundamentalism. The anti-war movement in the early to mid-2000s along with the climate justice movement also made contributions in forging more north-south movement linkages on issues not directly related to neoliberalism. The World Social Forum (WSF) process likely played an indirect role in expanding participation from Asia, Africa, and Latin America in global resistance to neoliberalism between the early 2000s and the early 2010s. The WSF largely organizes its core meetings in the global South with multiple subforums in countries in the global North and South.

[6] USA and Spain are considered "host countries" because the majority of actions on October 15, 2011 called for popular assemblies in the style of Occupy Wall Street and the Spanish Indignados at the height of their respective campaigns.

Table 6 Global economic justice movement major global days of action and geographic distribution of solidarity events in global South and North

Event and Date	Protest Events in Global South Outside of Host Country	Protest Events in Global North Outside of Host Country	Total
N30, WTO in Seattle, USA, November–December 1999	27 (23%)	92 (77%)	119 (100%)
S26, IMF/WB Prague, Czech Republic, September 2000	25 (24%)	81 (76%)	106 (100%)
J30, G8 Conference in Genoa, Italy, July 2001	25 (13%)	165 (87%)	190 (100%)
WTO Doha, Qatar November 2001	26 (21%)	96 (79%)	122 (100%)
WTO Cancun, 2003	43 (25%)	126 (75%)	169 (100%)
Global Day of Action, October 15, 2011 (no host countries)	224 (23%)	749 (77%)	973 (100%)
Global Day of Action, October 15, 2011 (with Spain and USA as host countries)	224 (34%)	426 (66%)	650 (100%)

Source: Created by the authors based on Almeida and Lichbach (2003), People's Global Action webpage, and https://15october.net.

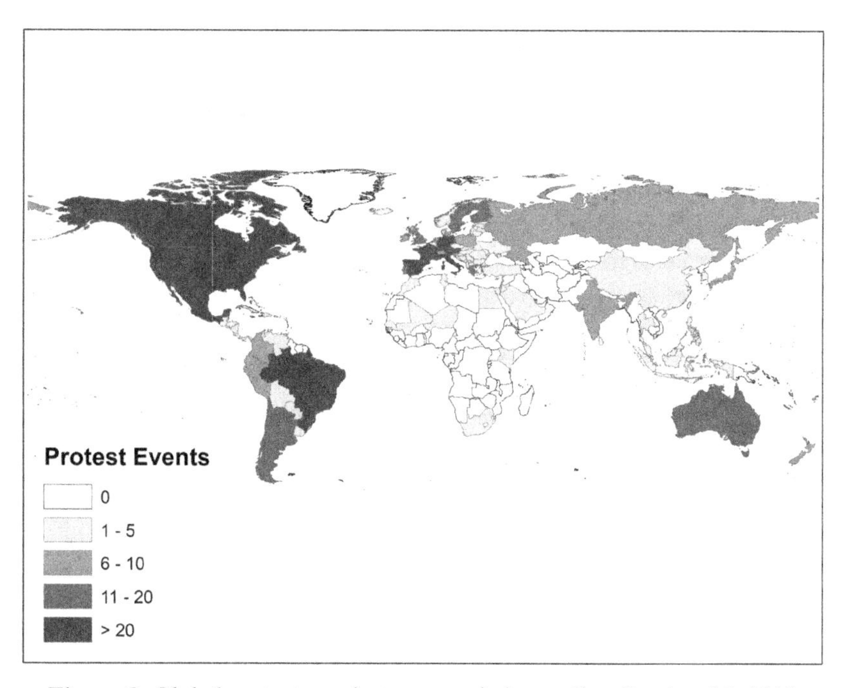

Figure 9 Global protests against economic inequality, October 15, 2011
Source: https://15october.net/reports.

World Social Forum as Coordinating Infrastructure in the Global South

With roots in the Partido de Los Trabajadores de Brasil, the World Social Forum (WSF; or *el Foro Social Mundial*, FSM in Spanish) acts as another significant step forward in promoting the mobilization against neoliberalism on a transnational scale. Since its founding assembly in Porto Alegre, Brazil, in 2001, it has quickly become the largest international gathering of progressive social activists seeking to resist neoliberal globalization and democratize the global economy (Reese et al., 2015; Smith, 2020). The initial World Social Forums were organized explicitly as counter-summits to the World Economic Forum (WEF) held annually in Geneva. The WEF provides an exclusive space where political and economic elites congregate to shape the global economic agenda within a neoliberal framework of expanding market fundamentalism. In contrast, the WSF encompasses "a set of forums – world, thematic, regional, sub-regional, national, municipal and local – that are organized according to its 'Charter of Principles'" (De Sousa Santos, 2004).

Besides the economic threats driving transnational protests, the timing of the upswing in coordination among movements and actors across nations in the global South in the late 2000s and 2010s, co-occurs with the growth of the WSF in global society. Between 2001 and 2018, the WSF convened international meetings on nearly an annual basis. From 2001 to 2003, the first three WSFs were held in Brazil (as well as in 2005, 2009, 2010, 2012, and 2018). Almost all of the principal WSFs have taken place in the global South, including India (2004); Venezuela, Mali, and Pakistan (2006); Kenya (2007); Senegal (2011); and Tunisia (2013 and 2015). Each WSF event attracted representation from well over one hundred nations, and the total combined participation at the main events reached more than 800,000 participants by 2016 (Fiedlschuster, 2018). Major related social forums, including subforums, have been held in the United States, Canada, Europe, Asia, the Caribbean, and throughout Latin America. When combining the international attendance at the main summits with the hundreds of thematic and subforums over the past twenty years, the global reach of the WSF is unprecedented for *movement* network connections across the global South.

Global Economic Justice Post-2020

The global economic justice movement was less active on the streets after the October 2011 actions. As a transnational movement in the contemporary era, it survives through the World Social Forum. Large protests continue outside of international financial meetings such as the G8 and G20, but without the hundreds of solidarity events (e.g., Hamburg 2017; Buenos Aires 2018) (Fischer, 2021). At the national level, massive popular outbursts and campaigns continue against the IMF, austerity, and economic inequality as observed in India and Costa Rica in 2020 and Tunisia, Ecuador, and Colombia in 2021–2022. The global climate justice movement (and increasingly, Fridays for Future) also takes on the transnational organizing template of the global economic justice movement in the 2010s and 2020s – holding a major event at a United Nations-sponsored climate policy summit (e.g., COP summit) combined with hundreds, and increasingly thousands of solidarity events around the globe. The planetary Covid pandemic appears to have dampened transnational actions, but not national-level uprisings against neoliberalism.

Other Transnational Movements Against Neoliberalism

Hemispheric Social Alliance Against FTAA

As neoliberal globalization intensified in Latin America during the 1990s through structural adjustment and deepening free trade initiatives that threaten state sovereignty and national labor protections, new and extensive forms of transnational activism appeared (Silva, 2013: 8). With the previous experience of the

North American Free Trade Agreement (NAFTA) treaty coming into force in 1994 and the rise of international Zapatismo (Andrews, 2011), a new complex of organizations, involving unions and NGOs in both the global North and South, focused on the economic threats associated with free trade treaties. This placed a transnational focus on the proposed Free Trade Area of the Americas (FTAA; or *Acuerdo de Libre Comercio para las Américas*, ALCA in Spanish) and its neoliberal model of governance (Anner and Evans, 2004).

The FTAA was an attempt at expansion of the NAFTA model of free trade to the entirety of thirty-four countries in North, Central, and South America and the Caribbean (with the exclusion of Cuba). Sustained transnational protests began against the FTAA in April 2001, during a third summit on the treaty in Quebec, Canada. An estimated 30,000 protesters demonstrated in the host city while dozens of solidarity events were held throughout North and South America. Other major days of transnational protest action against the FTAA occurred in 2002 and 2003 during official negotiations of potential member countries in Quito, Ecuador and Miami, Florida.

The most notable expression of these struggles is the Hemispheric Social Alliance (HSA; or *Alianza Social Continental*, ASC in Spanish), a broad transnational coalition constituted in 1997 (Anner and Evans, 2004; Von Bulow, 2010). Since the late 1990s, HSA carried out parallel people's summits and protests targeting the official presidential summits and ministerial meetings where high-level negotiations of the FTAA take place. As a result of the Santiago de Chile People's Summit of the Americas in 1998, HSA released its "Alternative for the Americas: Building a People's Hemispheric Agreement"[7] as a critical statement against neoliberalism. This "living document" called for a process of hemispheric consultation and dialogue on its proposed alternative vision of social integration and development. One of the most important actors of this alliance of alliances has been the Brazilian Network for the Integration of People (REBRIP). Also, the multisectoral Central de Trabajadores de la Argentina (CTA), played a crucial role in the protests that led to the final defeat of the FTAA in late 2005 (Rossi, 2013), along with women's movements.

International Women's Movement

The World March of Women (WMW) is a feminist, anti-neoliberal, and anti-racist women's movement seeking to eradicate structural causes of poverty and violence suffered by women. Early precedents for international women's day occurred in the 1910s and 1920s by socialist parties in the United States and

[7] This document is available here: www.iatp.org/sites/default/files/Alternatives_for_the_Americas_Building_a_Peopl.htm.

Europe supporting women's suffrage rights. In 1975, the United Nations officially proclaimed March 8 as International Women's Day (Puche i Moré, 2013). The WMW's first international meeting occurred in October 1998, but it was after the World March of Women in 2000 that the WMW became a permanent annual transnational action (in which eighty-nine nations participated), as agreed upon at the Third International Meeting in New Delhi, India, in 2003. In its twenty years of existence, the WMW has developed five International Actions guided by the mantra: *We resist to live, we march to transform!* According to its website, the WMW defines itself as "an autonomous, multicultural, multiethnic, pluralist and independent movement."[8] It is composed of fifty-eight National Coordinating Bodies (NCBs), active participant groups, and sympathizers. NCBs bring together active participating groups at the national level, particularly those from popular feminist organizations (Díaz Alba, 2021). They work around four action areas: the common good and public services; peace and demilitarization; violence against women; and women's economic autonomy.

The fight against neoliberalism and free trade agreements has been central to the WMW's agenda. One of its major goals is to challenge and denounce the policies and strategies of international financial, economic, and military institutions such as the IMF, the WTO, the WB, and transnational corporations that impoverish women and intensify the violence against them. Through alliances with other popular social movements, the WMW also aims to develop and implement feminist actions and alternatives to the commodification, exploitation, and degradation of natural resources and women's lives (Dufour and Giraud, 2007; Staggenborg and Lecomte, 2009). For instance, in 2015 the WNW joined several Latin American social movements in the *Jornada Continental por la Democracia y Contra el Neoliberalismo*.[9] In 2019, the WMW in Spain held a 24-hour strike backed by the main labor confederations and mobilized demonstrations in 500 Spanish cities and towns. More recently, in the context of Covid-19, at least twenty-two territories around the world conducted decentralized actions on March 8, 2021 to place "the sustainability of life on center stage," along with struggles "against neoliberalism, corporate power, and authoritarianism."[10] The transnational coordination of M8 marches and strikes have expanded the feminist repertoires of action while recovering

[8] WMW official website: https://marchemondiale.org.

[9] See, Sempreviva Organização Feminista and Marcha Mundial de las Mujeres (2017). *Desafíos Feministas para Enfrentar el Conflicto del Capital contra la Vida. Las Mujeres Seguimos en Lucha.* Sao Paulo: SOF.

[10] See, WMW March 8 Statement, 2021 at https://marchemondiale.org/index.php/2021/03/12/march-8-2021-feminist-resistance-to-put-the-sustainability-of-life-on-center-stage/.

historical roots of labor rights and class struggles (Torres Santana and Pérez Martín, 2021).

3 The Consequences of Resistance to Neoliberalism

Previous sections largely focused on the emergence of resistance to neoliberalism and its global diffusion. The present section takes on perhaps an even more consequential question: What are the outcomes and impacts of mobilization against neoliberalism over the short and long term? Although most of the protests studied here are about stopping a particular incursion – on the popular sectors or workers' rights – organizers also developed longer-term strategies directed to building political power through parties and electoral politics. We discuss both here. We analyze the conditions associated with successful campaigns in preventing the implementation of neoliberal policies. We also move from largely defensive mobilizing against unwanted economic policies and into the electoral sphere of cases where anti-neoliberal street battles led to the formation or expansion of political parties. These anti-neoliberal parties challenged the overall direction of free market priorities within city councils, regional governments, national legislatures, and at times, the executive branch.

Conditions Shaping the Outcomes of Anti-Neoliberal Protest Campaigns

The fundamental goal of anti-neoliberal campaigns focuses on preventing or turning back unwanted economic policies and protecting social citizenship rights. As Castells states, the conflict centers on political power,

> in any power relationship there is a certain degree of compliance and acceptance by those subjected to power. When resistance and rejection become significantly stronger than compliance and acceptance, power relationships are transformed: the terms of the relationship change, the powerful lose power, and ultimately there's a process of institutional change or structural change, depending on the extent of the transformation of power relationships (Castells, 2013: 11).

We have already covered when and where anti-neoliberal contention emerges as a sign of collective noncompliance and nonacceptance to market fundamentalism. Social movement theory also offers concrete explanations for the conditions under which "institutional change or structural change" is more likely to occur for less powerful groups – the second half of Castells's abstract formulation. Specifically, the vast literature on *social movement outcomes* provides guideposts into our understanding of the success and failures of campaigns resisting neoliberal policies. Amenta et al. (2018) suggest two primary means to examine social movement outcomes: 1) achievement of movement goals; and 2) gaining collective benefits for the constituency represented by the mobilization beyond explicitly stated goals. For this study, we emphasize the ability for campaigns to achieve relatively successful outcomes by obtaining their core goals (Burstein et al., 1995).

Some of the main conditions associated with successful outcomes for social movement campaigns in general include: specified goals; public opinion support; broad coalitions; larger numbers of participants; assertive tactics; resonant collective action frames; and effective neutralization or lack of countermovements (Almeida, 2019b). All of these conditions combined can be considered part of a highly dynamic and interactive institutional and multi-organizational field (Fligstein and McAdam, 2012; Klandermans, 1992; Ray, 2000; Useem and Goldstone, 2022). In addition, several of the elements driving campaign impacts provide some amount of agency to activists and organizers to shape the effectiveness of their struggles (e.g., specifying demands, messaging, reaching out to potential allies, and strategic choices at critical junctures). Campaign leaders need to read and interpret the organizational field and apply appropriate strategy (Ganz, 2009; Han et al., 2021).

Specified Goals: In most anti-neoliberal protest campaigns, demands are more specified, concrete, and singular than in other kinds of movements that often have multiple and abstract goals. The campaign often states "no" to the particular neoliberal measure in question as a simple binary choice. Even in the multiyear campaign against CAFTA in Costa Rica, the opposition referred to itself simply as the "No Campaign" or "No al TLC" (Raventós, 2018). Similarly, in other anti-neoliberal struggles the conflict revolves around if the privatization, subsidy cut, IMF agreement, or price increase is carried out by the state or not. This dichotomous outcome allows observers and researchers to more easily trace causal conditions to final results of campaign success or failure.

Favorable Public Opinion: Public opinion support is necessary to increase the likelihood of campaign success for multiple reasons. First, public opinion in support of a movement's goals assists activists in generating other favorable conditions in the field of contention such as broader coalitions, large numbers, and effective disruptive protest. Public opinion may most clearly be observed in representative surveys and polls on economic policies. Activists and leaders can also have good intuition regarding where the public mood stands on a particular market reform (Meyer, 2021: 26). Past experiences with neoliberal policies that did not end well for large segments of the population may also create favorable public opinion for an anti-neoliberal campaign in the present. This includes rising prices and poorer services from past economic reforms on public goods such as utilities, education, health care, public housing, and transportation, or corruption scandals from privatization.

Widespread public beliefs against free market reforms permit organizers to piece together broader coalitions from multiple sectors. The sympathy pool from which to draw participants is also much larger when a greater part of public opinion stands against the reforms. For example, based on representative sample polling since 2000, a majority of citizens in Latin America view privatization of the public sector unfavorably (Baker, 2009; McKenzie and Mookherjee, 2005). More assertive tactics (such as roadblocks) may also be perceived in a more positive light by the public (or at least the inconveniences tolerated) when large portions of society also prefer economic policies reversed or not implemented. The favorable public attitudes toward the campaign can help prevent severe state repression against mobilizations or create greater levels of contention if repression occurs. Finally, in relatively democratic contexts, lawmakers may fear heavy electoral losses when both public opinion and mobilized opposition challenge market reforms or austerity measures and eventually backpedal from their initial plans (as in India in 2021 with the deregulation of agricultural pricing).

Diverse Coalitions: Broad coalitions present a strong and united front against neoliberal measures. The alliances demonstrate to powerholders that multiple social sectors stand against the perceived economic threat. The perspective corresponds to Tilly's (1999) acronym for movement success of WUNC (public displays of worthiness, unity, numbers, and commitment). Indeed, social movement studies generally concur that threats assist in bringing different groups together in coalition (Reese et al., 2010; Staggenborg, 1986; Van Dyke and Amos, 2017). In privatization battles, the coalition may begin with the public sector workers in the affected area such as health care workers facing medical service privatization or utility workers in water, electricity, and telecommunications. These public employees are often already organized into labor unions or professional associations and may reach out to other public sector unions to widen the coalition in their campaign. In a study of 281 Latin American anti-austerity protest campaigns between 1995 and 2001, Almeida (2007: 129) found that public sector employees participated in nearly one in four campaigns.

With the absolute decline in labor unions over the past forty years, other sectors become vital to arranging broad coalitions. These sectors include education, health care, NGOs, environmental groups, feminist organizations, religious institutions, indigenous peoples, and oppositional political parties. Oppositional political parties, the educational system, and the health care system provide some of the limited number of organizational structures that are active throughout the *national territory* in the global South under neoliberalism. Hence, leftist political parties, schoolteachers, and health care workers may be key nodes in linking multiple groups together in larger oppositional networks to generate campaigns that operate in numerous geographic locations within a country. These wide coalitions that begin with the labor sector are often referred to as "social movement unionism" (Seidman, 1994). Labor union leaders in Costa Rica called this relationship "citizen unionism" (*sindicalismo ciudadano*) in the campaign against privatization and free trade.

Power in Numbers: Another condition associated with favorable outcomes in anti-neoliberal struggles involves the ability of organizers to bring out large numbers of demonstrators in public events opposing the economic policy (Somma and Medel, 2019). Similar to coalitions, huge crowds demonstrate widespread opposition to neoliberal measures and provide information to policymakers about the public mood of proposed or recently implemented changes such as privatization, structural adjustment, subsidy cuts, or price increases. High levels of civil society participation also assist in mobilizing events throughout the provinces beyond the capital city, and more people being potentially available to engage in assertive-type protest actions. Finally, the nature of neoliberalism as an economic threat, creates the possibility of mobilizing large numbers because people are more likely to join movements when facing losses versus the prospects of new advantages or gains (Bergstrand, 2014; Snow et al., 1998; Tilly, 1978).

Disruptive Protest: As stated at the beginning of this section, anti-neoliberal campaigns engage in asymmetrical power struggles over the future trajectory of social welfare. Most scholars incorporate the use of noninstitutional tactics in their definition of social movements (Staggenborg, 2022). Creative tactics such as large puppets (Wood, 2012) and other artistic expressions bring wider public awareness to the issue. The use of tactics such as roadblocks and occupations disrupt routine activities for economic and political elites (Gamson, 1975). At times, disruptive actions increase the bargaining leverage and likelihood of a favorable outcome via the recension of the neoliberal measure. The actual force of the disruptive protest can be observed in final written agreements between state representatives and oppositional groups whereby the government agrees to not implement the economic policy and activists accede to ending the confrontational tactic (e.g., roadblock, boycott, strike, occupation, etc.).

Inclusive Frames: Ideational components of a campaign complement favorable structural dimensions. Framing the anti-neoliberal struggle is fundamental in terms of defining the problem, assessing blame, and motivating widespread participation in ways that resonate with local beliefs and use familiar styles and idioms (Snow and Corrigal-Brown, 2005; Snow and Benford, 1988). The ability of activists to present the issue and cause in a fashion that appeals to the population in question is critical, especially in garnering public attention, recruiting participants in protest actions, and stitching together broad coalitions (Silva, 2009). In privatization battles, oppositional leaders often invoke symbols of patriotism and emphasize that selling off parts of the state infrastructure should be viewed as traitorous. Everyday public utilities such as the state water and aqueduct system, electrical distribution, and telecommunications become highlighted by oppositional groups as part of the national patrimony and belonging collectively to the citizenry.

When leading a campaign against privatization or free trade, organizers often appeal to social citizenship rights and populist nationalism. Their appeals especially gain traction through the use of protest music and other cultural expressions in the heat of struggle as witnessed in the 2019 Chilean uprising and the resurrection of Victor Jara songs in the streets during mass protest events. A cultural component accompanied the anti-CAFTA campaign in Costa Rica – the *movimiento cultural Frente al TLC*. Artists drove around the country in a rural school bus (*La Casadora*) and performed protest music and other performative acts to denounce the free trade agreement (Raventós, 2018).

Countermovements: When elite or other conservative political actors organize countercampaigns in favor of neoliberal measures, it places obstacles on the focal campaign (Meyer and Staggenborg, 1996). Because austerity and privatization policies are usually unpopular across a wide spectrum of civil society, from low-income groups to the middle class, organized *pro-neoliberal* campaigns are less common. They are most likely to occur when there is a relatively longer timeline to debate a particular policy – from a few months to a few years. Pro-neoliberal crusades have taken place over free trade treaties. Local economic elites that benefit from unregulated foreign investment, such as in the banking, tourism, resource extraction, or export manufacturing sectors, may finance publicity campaigns in favor of free trade or liberalizing measures that, at times, even involve street mobilizations. This involves clientelist-type networks of owners or managers pressuring workers in the international sector of the economy to participate in countercampaigns (e.g., export processing zone workers). Countermovements challenge movement frames and may influence public opinion in favor of repressive responses to the focal anti-neoliberal protest campaigns, making success more difficult (Fernandez, 2008; Inclán, 2012).

While any of these conditions individually increase the power of an anti-neoliberal campaign, they do seem to have an even greater impact if combined. When anti-neoliberal struggles mobilize large numbers in diverse coalitions, use effective framing strategies that influence public opinion, employ disruptive repertoires, and avoid countercampaigns, we would expect more favorable outcomes, especially in democratic states.

Anti-Neoliberal Campaign Outcomes in the Global North

We can observe the conditions for campaign success activated in real world collective struggles against the implementation of market fundamentalism and the erosion of citizenship rights. In the global North, most attention on neoliberal policy outcomes comes from studies of welfare reform and privatization in North America and the Great Recession and Eurocrisis in Europe. Scholars also pay attention to labor conflicts against the global restructuring of manufacturing and the historical abandonment of Fordist labor relations (Moody, 1997; Martin, 2008), low wages in segments of the service sector (e.g., Fight for $15), and teachers' strikes against declining benefits and wages (Blanc, 2021; Pullum, 2020).

The Clinton Administration's Personal Responsibility and Work Opportunity Reconciliation Act (PRWORA) of 1996 allowed for the privatization of welfare services at the state and local level throughout the United States. Reese (2011), in a comparison of city-level campaigns, shows that the mobilizations with greater support among public sector unions, welfare rights organizations, and community associations were able to hold back privatization of the Temporary Assistance for Needy Families (TANF) program. Only 25 percent of TANF was privatized in Los Angeles, while local leaders privatized the entire TANF program in Milwaukee. Campaigns in both Los Angeles and Milwaukee used disruptive protest in labor and community coalitions, but only Los Angeles had a favorable political environment where activists could influence the county board of supervisors, while Milwaukee's welfare laws remained at the state level and impervious to the anti-privatization campaign.

Other anti-neoliberal battles in the global North involve water privatization. In an exhaustive and detailed comparison of water privatization in Stockton, California and Vancouver, Canada, Robinson (2013) highlights some of the central dimensions shaping neoliberal policy outcomes. In Stockton, in the early 2000s, a community-level campaign attempted to prevent the privatization of municipal water services. The anti-privatization coalition consisted of environmentalists, students, municipal water workers, and voting rights activists. The coalition suffered from internal diagnostic framing disputes and decided to mobilize around an institutionalized strategy of a referendum instead of mass disruption. The city's mayor also organized a pro-privatization countermovement. Even though the referendum was successful, the city approved the privatization and a major multinational water administration firm (OMI-Thames) took over the city services for five years until courts ruled in favor of the oppositional coalition and returned water administration back to municipal control.

In contrast, in Vancouver in 2001, a community campaign was able to halt an attempt at the privatization of a major water filtration project in a relatively short time period – the largest proposed public-private partnership in Canadian history. The anti-privatization alliance included a wide diversity of community-based organizations, environmentalists, labor unions, and national and international social movements. The campaign used both creative and disruptive tactics and effectively framed the privatization efforts to local misgivings about NAFTA, international free trade, and the loss of local control. Water administration and filtration remained under local public control, and the campaign succeeded by achieving its central goal – preventing the privatization (Robinson, 2013). Similarly, in the late 2010s, a wide coalition of environmental, labor, women's health, racial justice, and community-based organizations in Pittsburgh used creative public awareness tactics and the resonant frame of "citizens' rights to water" to prevent the city from returning to private contractors for water administration as it had during the 2008 Great Recession and municipal indebtedness (González Rivas and Schroering, 2021).

In Europe, a parallel struggle took place in the French city of Grenoble between 1989 and 2000. A coalition of civic and ecology associations successfully overturned an earlier privatization and returned water and sewage services to municipal control (Barlow and Clarke, 2002). During the Eurocrisis of 2011, Portugal and Greece came under enormous pressure to privatize local water administration to reduce their respective national debts. In Greece, a broad alliance between water administration labor unions and social movements fighting austerity (a form of social movement unionism) successfully reversed major water privatization initiatives in Thessaloniki and Athens in the 2010s. In Portugal, labor unions formed a narrow alliance with the Portuguese Communist Party, and only had the capacity to block privatization in cities with a leftist city government (Bieler and Jordan, 2018).

By comparing water privatization campaigns in the global North greater insight is gained into the outcomes of anti-neoliberal resistance. We observe longer and relatively less successful struggles when campaigns face countermovements, develop conflicting frames, construct narrow coalitions, and/or fail to employ creative and disruptive tactics (e.g., Stockton and Portugal). The more successful campaigns constructed resonant frames, coordinated wide and diverse coalitions, and engaged in assertive and novel tactics (e.g., Vancouver, Pittsburgh, Grenoble, Thessaloniki, and Athens).

The cases compared here concerning welfare, labor, and water rights act as a microcosm for much of the global North, where the best that campaigns can do is try to hold back the tide of the ongoing spread of neoliberalism. In the global South, we find more successful cases of short- to medium-term victories in defeating austerity, privatization, and free trade, while at the same time acknowledging that there are many more cases of *non-mobilization* and failed campaigns (Auyero and Swistun, 2009).

Anti-Neoliberal Campaign Outcomes in the Global South

Between the 1990s and 2010s dozens of major campaigns took place throughout the Central American isthmus against specific neoliberal measures. To avoid over-sampling on the dependent variable (i.e., observing only cases with campaign success), it is critical to analyze campaigns over time and/or across campaigns and countries that include instances of failed struggles. In one study, Almeida (2008) compared four anti-neoliberal campaigns in Costa Rica and El Salvador. Two campaigns were unsuccessful and two campaigns achieved their goals. The failed campaign in Costa Rica took place in 1995 over structural adjustment that would raise the retirement age for teachers and reduce their pensions, cut subsidies on a number of consumer goods for the general public, result in the dismissal of 8,000 public sector workers, and implement a regressive sales tax. Mass mobilizations took place for over a month and mostly involved teachers and public sector workers. In the end the movement failed, and the government implemented the measures. The successful campaign in Costa Rica occurred in 2000 over the privatization of electricity and telecommunications, discussed in Section 2. In this campaign activists created much wider coalitions and used even more disruptive tactics with the use of the roadblock and the legislature scrapped its plans for the privatization.

In El Salvador, between 1994 and 1997, as part of a larger World Bank sponsored "state modernization" program, the pro-business government of President Armando Calderón Sol moved to privatize state telecommunications – ANTEL. The ANTEL workers and other public sector allies attempted to mobilize against the privatization, but in the end lost. An even larger campaign erupted between 1999 and 2003 to stop the privatization of the social security hospitals in the Salvadoran health system. In this struggle, medical doctors and staff created broad alliances with the main oppositional political party and a diversity of civil society organizations, and prevented the outsourcing of medical services on two separate occasions. The health care campaign also used mass marches and dozens of highway roadblocks, and occupied worksites.

Three major differences between the successful campaigns and the failed campaigns include: 1) high levels of external solidarity in protest events; 2) heavy use of disruptive protests outside of the capital city; and 3) organizational learning from prior defeats. In the successful anti-privatization campaigns in Costa Rica and El Salvador, there was widespread support from diverse social sectors. Indeed, labor unions in the affected sectors in both countries established multisectoral umbrella organizations at the beginning of the successful campaigns to formalize alliances with external allies (e.g., *Movimiento Cívico Nacional* and the *Liga Cívica* in Costa Rica and the *Foro de la Sociedad Civil* and the *Alianza Ciudadana contra la Privatización* in El Salvador). With these new alliances, the level of solidarity increased substantially in the successful campaigns. In the failed 1995 campaign in Costa Rica, only 31 percent of protest events included groups other than schoolteachers. In the 2000 anti-privatization campaign in Costa Rica, more than two-thirds of all protest events (68 percent) included multiple sectors. In El Salvador, in the unsuccessful campaign to prevent telecommunications privatization only 31 percent involved outside groups. In the two successful anti-health care privatization campaigns, 72 percent and 64 percent of all protest events, respectively, included sectors outside of social security.

Very few disruptive protests occurred in the failed campaigns, while the two successful campaigns were characterized by roadblocks, solidarity strikes, and occupations. In Costa Rica alone, 51 percent of all protest events in the anti-privatization campaign involved obstructing traffic. In the final negotiations in both of the triumphant campaigns labor union leaders agreed to stop striking and blocking roads in exchange for the cessation of the privatization initiatives. As a clear sign of the strategic power of highway and road barricades for subaltern groups, in the years immediately following the successful anti-privatization campaigns, the parliaments in both countries passed legislation banning roadblocks, making them a serious criminal offense (Almeida, 2012).

Both successful campaigns came immediately after failed attempts to prevent neoliberal policy implementation. Organizational learning had occurred for activists between the two campaigns. This sequencing of campaigns helps us understand the adjustments activists might make between collective struggles. The public mood may change as well from one campaign to another. For example, in El Salvador, the public felt the price increases immediately after the first round of privatizations in the late 1990s. Activists took advantage of public sentiments and learned from failed strategies to form larger multisectoral coalitions in the next more successful round of anti-neoliberal struggles.

Several other cases in Latin American illustrate how the conditions for positive outcomes are activated. Panama followed a similar path of organizational learning and coalition building as the Costa Rican and Salvadoran cases. By 1995, nearly a third of Panama's budget went to pay off its foreign debt. Telecommunications and energy had already been privatized after campaign defeats in the early 1990s. In 1995, the Panamanian government implemented a new labor flexibility law that labor unions, led by the militant construction workers' union, SUNTRACS, resisted with a massive two-week strike. More than 300 workers were arrested, and five workers were killed in the struggle, and the movement failed to prevent the legislation. Nonetheless, activists in the organizational field demonstrated experiential learning from the losses and much wider coalitions were constructed for the next campaign against major neoliberal legislation in 1998 – the attempt at water privatization.

Between the defeat of 1995 and the initiation of the 1998 campaign in Panama, new semiformal coalitions were formed, including the *Confederación Nacional de Unidad Sindical Independiente* (CONUSI) (composed of 49 labor unions with experience in the 1995 labor flexibility strike) and the multisectoral *Movimiento Nacional por la Defensa de la Soberanía* (MONADESO). During the 1998 campaign, students, public and private sector labor organizations, and schoolteachers worked together to hold events in multiple locations and prevent the privatization of the state water administration institute (IDAAN). From this success, organizers assembled an even broader coalition between 2003 and 2005 to prevent the restructuring and partial privatization of the social security hospital and pension system – the Panamanian Caja de Seguro Social.

Panamanian activists entitled the coalition the National Front in Defense of Social Security (FRENADESSO). The broad coalition was composed of CONUSI, SUNTRACS, physicians, staff, and clients of the social security system, university and high school student associations, schoolteachers' unions, and community-based organizations. FRENADESSO led two campaigns, in 2003 and 2005, to prevent the neoliberal restructuring of the Panamanian health and retirement systems. The two campaigns were both successful and prevented the restructuring in the medium term. To date, these campaigns still register as the largest in modern Panamanian history. Hence, we see in several instances in Central America during the height of privatizations in the 1990s and early 2000s, that less successful campaigns maintain more narrow coalitions and were more likely to occur in the first wave of privatizations advised by IFIs. Local labor leaders and progressive NGOs learned from the earlier defeats and developed novel multisectoral templates with assertive repertoires to turn back privatization and outsourcing in some of the most valued public institutions and welfare state services in the region.

Other successful campaigns in Latin America showed similar dynamics in terms of the widespread use of the roadblock combined with diverse coalitions such as the defeat of the Ecuador-United States Free Trade Agreement in 2006 (Ramírez Gallegos, 2011), the anti-electricity privatization in Arequipa, Peru in 2002 (Arce, 2008), and the battles against water and natural gas privatization in Bolivia between 1999 and 2005. More recently, multisectoral coalitions prevented price hikes resulting from an IMF agreement in Ecuador in October 2019 after twelve days of massive unrest by indigenous peoples, women, students, transportation workers, and labor unions (Moreno et al., 2021). In mid-2019, the Honduran government attempted a combined partial privatization of the national health care and national education systems – two of the most organized sectors in neoliberal Latin America. From April to June, the newly created coalition *Plataforma de Defensa de la Salud y la Educación Pública* coordinated protests for sixty days. The high points came on May 30–31 and June 17–19 bringing the country to a standstill on both occasions. Sosa (2019) reports 130 roadblocks across the country in late May alone (see Figure 10). The massive disruptive protest campaign forced the government of Juan Orlando Hernández to back down and cancel the privatization and restructuring plans.

In addition to broad coalitions and the use of mass disruption, all of the previously discussed successful campaigns in Latin America also benefited or incorporated several other conditions associated with favorable outcomes. They all involved large demonstrations and used inclusive framing strategies that emphasized the economic threats posed by the neoliberal reforms for large segments of the population. Some of these successful campaigns also enjoyed favorable public opinion and largely avoided well-organized countermovements. Other labor and community coalitions have merged together in Africa to prevent water privatization in Nigeria as well as municipal-level energy privatization in South Africa. At the same time, a twenty-year-long campaign took place over municipal water privatization in Jakarta, Indonesia, but faced a sustained elite countermovement that prevented a decisive victory of remunicipalization (Lobina et al., 2019). At the transnational level, the survival and maintenance of the global economic justice movement and the WSF can also be viewed as a relatively positive outcome.

From Defensive to Offensive Mobilization: Electoral Outcomes

Besides the immediate mobilization outcomes of defensive campaigns to turn back unwanted economic changes and policies, under extraordinary circumstances, oppositional groups have converted anti-neoliberal struggles into *anti-neoliberal parties* with varying levels of electoral success. That is, oppositional movements have moved from defensive struggles to turn back unwanted market reforms to offensive struggles through entering elections to increase their

Figure 10 Photo of march of Plataforma de Defensa de la Salud y la Educación Pública, 2019 in Honduras (Photo credit: Paul Carvajal)

political power. There are some examples as early as 1978 with Peru's constitutional convention producing gains for several left parties (Roberts, 1998). The Peruvian example at the dawn of the neoliberal era outlined a trend repeated throughout Latin America and southern Europe for the next forty years – *an anti-neoliberal protest wave followed by left party electoral success* (see Table 7).

In political science and sociology scholars increasingly show an interest in understanding the relationships between social movements and political parties

(Tarrow, 2021). For the purposes of this study, the starting point involves the conversion of social movement-type mobilization into electoral mobilization. Scholars studying movements and parties find the relationship complex and multidirectional (McAdam and Tarrow, 2010). This makes causal claims difficult in that the alliance between parties and movements is often reciprocal. Protest campaigns provide oppositional parties with central issues for their platforms and a base of volunteers to help get out the vote. In exchange, political parties provide protest campaigns with a national organizational structure with local chapters spread across the geographical territory that can call out their party members and militants to support a protest drive. Parties with some institutional representation can also usher in demands of protest campaigns into the legislative branch of government to prevent unwanted economic changes. In the neoliberal era, with the weakening of labor unions, the public sector, and large rural cooperatives, political parties are one of the few national-level organizational entities that may coordinate with social movements (Almeida, 2010). Despite these obstacles to deciphering causal determinacy, anti-neoliberal resistance tends to, at least initially, begin with a sequential pattern in terms of growing electoral power.

Before transitioning into a serious competitive electoral party contender with a strong anti-neoliberal platform, some type of protest campaign or protest wave usually occurs first. People can congregate immediately over an unwanted economic measure using everyday settings and organizations such as schools, workplaces, neighborhood, and village ties. Forming or aligning with a political party to overturn free market fundamentalism in the legislature through an electoral challenge has a longer time horizon and often builds its core support from a prior anti-neoliberal mobilization in the streets and highways. A large protest campaign offers a fungible infrastructure to build a potent electoral party around rejecting neoliberal policies in several dimensions, including barometers, frames, volunteers, and organizing experience.

An efficacious campaign against free trade, austerity, privatization, or structural adjustment acts as a signal to electoral challengers that market fundamentalism may be an issue to galvanize political party support. Campaigns or protest waves that are successful, long-lasting, and mobilize large numbers across the country demonstrate the electoral potential and viability of anti-neoliberalism as a central plank in an oppositional party platform. Anti-neoliberal protest campaigns also produce novel understandings to show the general public what free market policies entail and why they may be harmful. Sustained mobilizations produce cultural artifacts of protest songs and slogans that simplify the problems associated with labor force flexibility, privatization, price increases, and free trade that can be used again in the future for other purposes, including election campaigns. Finally, large-scale anti-neoliberal protest waves produce new communities and populations with extensive organizing experience that can also be used as volunteers in later election campaigns to canvas door-to-door and get out the vote for a progressive oppositional party (Almeida et al., 2021). Multisectoral coalitions and organizations often coordinate extensive protest campaigns and waves providing an established infrastructure to like-minded oppositional parties. All of these dimensions require a relatively democratic context to operate.

Democratic and competitive elections provide one necessary condition for a protest campaign to transition into an electoral campaign. Activists usually have three options to continue anti-neoliberal goals through electoral politics: 1) form a new anti-neoliberal party; 2) align in elections with a small oppositional party already in existence; or 3) align with a large traditional oppositional party already in existence (Della Porta et al., 2017). Parties in power are usually not interested in aligning with movements as a *new enterprise after they have taken power* because of budget constraints and the uncertainties brought about by disruptive protests (Bruhn, 2008). In many contexts, a large opposition party with an interest in contesting the deepening of neoliberalization is not an option. Hence, in most cases, activists from anti-neoliberal protest campaigns may attempt to launch a new anti-neoliberal electoral party or align with smaller oppositional parties already in existence. Next, we illustrate these dynamics with several examples from Latin America and southern Europe.

The Protest Wave Path to Strong Electoral Outcomes in Latin America

Peru: As mentioned earlier, between 1976 and 1978 several mass strikes and large demonstrations took place against the Peruvian military government's austerity program, which was seeking a loan from the IMF. When the country transitioned toward democratization in 1978, the government held elections for a constitutional assembly. Five leftist parties competed in the constitutional assembly that had participated in the 1976–8 anti-austerity protest waves and gained nearly 30 percent of the total vote (29.5 percent). Roberts (1998: 219–220), summarizes the significance of these results as, "This was nearly ten times the vote obtained by the Left in the last national elections in 1963 and the highest vote ever obtained by a Marxist Left in Latin America outside of Chile." Hence, the case of Peru provided an indicator of what was to come in the neoliberal period under a system of *relatively* competitive elections. More recently, Peru's presidential elections in 2021 were won by the leftist LIBRE party and the new president (Pedro Castillo) served as the main union leader in a 2017 national teachers' strike over wages that endured for several months. Pedro Castillo campaigned throughout the country carrying a gigantic 10-foot pencil, reminding voters the importance of public education (and the public sector in general) in the path to his unprecedented victory.

Brazil: The Brazilian Workers' Party (PT) provides another template in how to convert anti-neoliberal mobilization into sustained electoral power. In particular, *the PT showed that social movement-type resources were just as powerful as the conventional economic assets used by dominant and traditional political parties*. Indeed, Keck (1992: 238–239) succinctly states the following about the Brazilian Workers' Party: "by 1988 political commentators counted the party's ability to call upon its activists for social and political campaigns as a political resource that almost made up for its lack of financial resources." Labor union leaders established The Workers' Party in Brazil at the dawn of neoliberalism in 1980. The party's first takeoff point occurred after a series of strikes and protests against inflation in 1988 while the PT called for an end to debt payments and relations with the IMF in its party platform. In the 1988 local elections, the PT won the mayorships of thirty large cities (including Sao Paulo) and 1,000 municipal council seats (up from 179 in 1985) (Sader and Silverstein, 1991: 99). The Workers' Party took this momentum into 1989 with a continued strike wave against the government's third austerity program against inflation. The PT catapulted to the second largest party in the country, only losing in the runoff presidential elections in December 1989 by 4 million votes (31 million to 35 million). The first two planks of the PT's 1989 presidential platform called for an end to paying interest on the foreign debt and halting privatizations. From this huge leap forward, the PT would remain the largest opposition party until winning the presidency in 2002 and holding it until 2016. While in executive power, the PT implemented a number of anti-neoliberal measures, including participatory budgeting, land reforms, and the *Bolsa Familia* cash transfer program to low-income families, among many other initiatives.

Uruguay: The Frente Amplio Party formed in the country before authoritarian rule in 1971 and reemerged with the return of democracy in the mid-1980s to immediately align with anti-neoliberal movements (Bidegain and Tricot, 2017). The leftist opposition party continued to gain electoral support with each election cycle until winning the presidency in 2004. In 1992, the Frente Amplio mobilized with the Inter-Union Workers' Federation-National Workers' Convention (PIT-CNT) to successfully reject a national referendum allowing the privatization of state enterprises. In the 1990s, the Frente Amplio also aligned with pensioner movements and teachers' unions through the organization of national plebiscites (Bidegain and Tricot, 2017). The left party also built strong relationships with the urban poor that engaged in squatter movements and land invasions (Álvarez-Rivadulla, 2017). The final jump in electoral success occurred between 2002 and 2004 when the leftist party supported the campaign against water privatization. The water privatization campaign mobilized throughout the national territory until winning a plebiscite in 2004 on the same day as national elections whereby the Frente Amplio won the presidency. The Frente Amplio electoral turnout in the 2004 victory was especially strong in regions with high protest activity in the water privatization campaign (Almeida, 2010). After winning the 2004 elections, the Frente Amplio continued to win the executive branch until 2019 with two additional presidential election victories. The 2004 elections also gave the Frente Amplio a majority in the bicameral congress for the first time and dissolved a 175-year tradition of elite party dominance by the Colorado and Blanco parties (Luna, 2007).

Nicaragua: In the 1980s after the overthrow of the Somoza dictatorship, the revolutionary movement (the Frente Sandinista para la Liberación Nacional – FSLN) converted into a political party. The FSLN lost elections in 1990 and became an oppositional party. For the next sixteen years it aligned with anti-neoliberal movements over austerity, land and water privatization, university budgets, and public transportation fares to build enough power to win back major cities, parliamentary seats, and eventually the presidency in late 2006.

El Salvador: Similar to Nicaragua, a revolutionary movement emerged in the 1970s fighting an extremely repressive military government. The revolutionary Frente Farabundo Martí para la Liberación Nacional (FMLN), converted into an oppositional political party after the peace accords in 1992. The party moved from being the third largest oppositional party to the largest through several anti-neoliberal protest campaigns in the late 1990s and early 2000s, the most important confrontations being the struggle against health care privatization and free trade. After the two campaigns against health care privatization between 1999 and 2003, the party had gained the second largest number of seats in parliament. Between 2004 and 2008, the FMLN continued to align with movements in the streets and send its 80,000 party members into protests to battle the Central America Free Trade Agreement (CAFTA) and water privatization until winning the executive branch in 2009, and again in 2014.

Honduras: Anti-neoliberal campaigns trace back to the early 1990s during the first wave of structural adjustment. After signing two structural adjustment agreements with the World Bank between 1988 and 1990 (which included eighteen conditionality requirements), President Callejas implemented a number of austerity and privatization measures in 1990 and 1992, including currency devaluation, state sector selloffs, and the privatization of land reform farms. The neoliberal measures sparked the largest wave of protests in decades between 1990 and 1992, involving rural workers, public health workers, and state sector employees (Sosa, 2013). At the time, there was no left party that could convert the anti-neoliberal discontent into electoral success.

In the early 2000s, the Honduran state issued a new series of austerity and privatization measures, including attempts at water privatization. The measures came from three IMF agreements signed between 1999 and 2004, but faced a new wave of oppositional protest. One high point for the oppositional forces in civil society involved the creation in 2003 of the Coordinadora Nacional de Resistencia Popular (CNRP). Between 2004 and 2009, the CNRP held multiple national campaigns against neoliberal policies, including water privatization and CAFTA. The CNRP also worked with a newly legalized left-leaning political party – Unificación Democrática (UD). In both the 2001 and 2005 parliamentary elections, the UD won five legislative seats, and several of the representatives were also social movement leaders and advocated against further neoliberal reforms inside the state.

After a military coup in 2009, the new regime went on a more aggressive neoliberal path creating special economic zones for foreign investors and opening up mining and agricultural lands to transnational capital. The CNRP converted into the Frente Nacional de Resistencia Popular (FNRP) to organize against the coup and latest phase of neoliberal reforms. Eventually the FNRP evolved into the Libertad y Refundación (LIBRE) political party in 2013. In the 2013 presidential elections, the LIBRE party gained nearly 900,000 votes and displaced the 100-year-old biparty system of the Liberal and National Parties by coming in second place. The UD party only gained around 25,000 votes for the presidency in 2001 and 2005, but the resistance on the streets by the CNRP and FNRP transformed the LIBRE party into a serious electoral contender. Between 2013 and 2021, LIBRE continued as the second largest party in Honduras and likely won the presidency in 2017 but was blocked after election irregularities allowed the Partido Nacional to remain in power.[11] LIBRE supported the 2019 protest campaign against health care and educational privatization (described earlier) and eventually triumphed in the 2021 national elections with the country's first woman president – Xiomara Castro – and a plurality of legislative seats.

Bolivia: The Asamblea por la Soberanía de los Pueblos (ASP), Movement Toward Socialism (MAS), and the Movimiento Indígena Pachakuti (MIP) began as indigenous-based parties with the change in local and national electoral laws in the 1990s making it easier for smaller parties to compete. MIP and

[11] See Organization of American States-sponsored study of 2017 presidential election returns at, www.oas.org/fpdb/press/Nooruddin-Analysis-for-OAS-Honduras-2017.pdf.

MAS also incorporated "movement" into their official party names. The small left-leaning indigenous parties garnered about 3 percent of the vote in local and national elections between 1995 and 1999. In the early 2000s, after major neoliberal battles over water privatization and regressive taxation (as well as rural battles over coca production, land reform, and indigenous rights), the small left parties strengthened in the 2002 national elections. Combined, MIP and MAS gained 27 percent of the national vote, with MIP winning six representatives in the Chamber of Deputies, and the MAS winning twenty-seven deputies and eight senators (Van Cott, 2007). High-profile social movement leaders served as party legislative representatives (e.g., Evo Morales, José Bailaba, Román Loayza Caero, and Felipe Quispe) (Van Cott, 2007).

After the 2002 elections, national level protest campaigns coordinated with the MAS and MIP parties to demand nationalization of gas reserves and operations, and greater taxation on foreign extraction. The MAS party activists were especially adept at blending urban and rural struggles against neoliberalism into single platforms (Anria, 2018). After two especially massive and nationwide protest campaigns over natural gas policies, in 2003 and 2005, the MAS won the executive branch with the country's first indigenous president and with the largest margin of victory in the modern era. The MAS also won a majority of seats in the national Chamber of Deputies and nearly half of the Senate seats. In 2006, within months of taking office, President Morales nationalized the oil and gas industry. The MAS held on to power until 2019, and then triumphed again in the presidential and parliamentary elections in 2021.

Ecuador: The indigenous-based oppositional party Pachakutik built electoral power in the 1990s and 2000s in protests against neoliberalism – including major national campaigns against structural adjustment and free trade that shut the country down for days at a time via demonstrations and roadblocks (Becker, 2011). Specifically, Movimiento de Unidad Plurinacional Pachakutik – Nuevo País was created in 1995 after a countrywide protest campaign against President Durán Ballén's agrarian development law seeking to privatize land and water in rural and indigenous territories in 1994 (Van Cott, 2007; Pérez Martín, 2016). Pachakutik formed alliances with major indigenous federations and urban social movements (in the Coordinadora de Movimientos Sociales – CMS). After declining electoral success in the mid-2000s, Pachakutik gave support to Rafael Correa and his newly formed Alianza PAIS (Patria Altiva i Soberana) party in the second round of presidential voting in 2006. Correa earned a PhD from the University of Illinois in economics and his dissertation critiqued the Washington Consensus policies of the World Bank and IMF (Becker, 2011). Major anti-free trade protests led by the indigenous movement between 2004 and 2006 before the presidential elections likely played a major role in mobilizing the necessary vote totals to bring the first anti-neoliberal government into power (Ramírez Gallegos, 2011). Alianza PAIS remained in power with majority representation in the national parliament until 2017.

Venezuela: Hugo Chávez built his electoral road to power in concert with smaller left parties that battled neoliberalism. The package of IMF reforms implemented in Venezuela in 1989 unleashed a wave of protests (including the *Caracazo*), riots, and coup attempts in the following decade – a reported 5,000 protest events (Silva, 2009). Oppositional political parties such as *La Causa Я* and Hugo Chávez's Revolutionary Bolivarian Movement (MBR-200/MVR) blamed the IFI "paquetes" for many of the country's social problems (López Maya, 2005) – often referring to the economic policies as *neoliberalismo salvaje* (savage neoliberalism). The Christian Democratic government of Rafael Caldera signed a particularly harsh IMF structural adjustment agreement in 1996. The accord called for raising consumer prices on basic goods and transportation as well as privatization in a number of industries. The period from 1996 to 1997 involved large-scale protests and strikes led by public sector unions, with multiple mass actions of more than a million protest participants against the structural adjustment measures (Silva, 2009). Opposition parties, such as La Causa Я also participated in the protests via their affiliated unions (Silva, 2009). These same oppositional parties would culminate in Chavez's new Movimiento Quinta República (MVR) coalitional party (established in 1997) that incorporated La Causa Я and the Movement toward Socialism (MAS). The MVR went on to electoral victory in late 1998 with 56 percent of the popular vote (Gates, 2010; López Maya, 2005). The coalition evolved into the Partido Socialista de Venezuela (PSUV) and has remained in power since 1999.

Paraguay: After massive anti-privatization protests in Paraguay in the early to mid-2000s (Riquelme, 2004), led by the Frente Nacional de Defensa de Bienes Publicas y la Soberanía, a coalition of small opposition parties and social movements came together in a new party – the Patriotic Alliance for Change. The new political force won the presidential elections in 2008 with Fernando Lugo as the candidate (a former Catholic Bishop inspired by liberation theology).

Mexico: Andrés Manuel López Obrador's new MORENA party in Mexico won the presidential elections in 2018 on the heels of a massive protest campaign (the *Gasolinazo*) against the deregulation of the state petroleum institute (PEMEX). MORENA also won both houses of Congress. AMLO previously affiliated with the Partido Revolucionario Democrático (PRD) as mayor of Mexico City and two-time presidential candidate. The PRD had also grown in strength in the 1990s and 2000s aligning with social movements against austerity (Cadena-Roa and Alonso, 2004).

Chile: In the early 2010s, the Frente Amplio party emerged out of the student protests over tuition costs and a partially privatized education system. The new leftist party elected four student activists into parliament in the national elections of 2013 (Donoso and Somma, 2021) and went on to win twenty-four seats in the 2017 national elections. The Frente Amplio grew in strength after the October 2019 anti-neoliberal uprising that forced a new a constitutional convention. In the 2021 Constituent Assembly Election the Frente Amplio won the second most votes and seats in the assembly, along with several other progressive currents. The Frente Amplio also used the momentum and energy of the 2019 mass mobilizations to win the presidency in late 2021 in the Social Convergence coalition. The newly elected president, Gabriel Boric, had served as a leader in the early student protests. A similar sequencing of events occurred in Colombia of anti-neoliberal protests and electoral gains between 2019 and 2022 eventuating in the historic presidential and vice presidential victory of the Pacto Histórico.

The Protest Wave Path to Strong Electoral Outcomes in Southern Europe

In the global North, Spain and Greece exemplified the neoliberal protest to electoral success pathway in the 2010s. In Spain, the massive protest wave was initiated in 2010 against the austerity measures of the Zapatero government in the context to the Great Recession. Zapatero moved to reform pensions, cut salaries, and implement a new labor flexibility law. The economic measures were met with mass protests and the first general strike in eight years (Della Porta et al., 2017). The anti-neoliberal resistance received a huge boost on May 15, 2011 with the occupation of public squares by ordinary citizens across the country that became known as *the indignados* and the M-15 movement against austerity and housing costs. Activists initially organized the M-15 via social media platforms. The M-15 movement campaign converted into the formation of a new political party – Podemos. Podemos was established in 2014 by leaders of the indignado anti-austerity campaigns and used territorial chapters across the country called Podemos Circles (Flesher Fominaya, 2020b). In the 2014 European parliamentary elections, Podemos received more than 5 million votes and five seats (Flesher Fominaya, 2020b). In the 2015 national legislative elections, Podemos won the third most seats in congress (forty-nine) and twelve seats in the senate. Podemos also worked with other smaller parties to win representation in provincial governments and municipal power in major cities such as Madrid, Barcelona, Valencia, Zaragoza, La Coruña, and Cádiz.

In Greece, the Syriza party came out of a coalition of leftist parties and organizations in the early 2000s. The party was built out of struggles against privatization and market-oriented reforms to the national social security and pension systems. The small opposition party slowly won seats in parliament in the 2000s. By 2010, with the Greek debt crisis and forced austerity by the European Commission, European Central Bank, and the IMF, poverty and unemployment rates climbed rapidly, while health and social services suffered severe cutbacks. The extreme economic crisis in Greece led to greater levels of mass mobilization. Between 2010 and 2012 twenty general strikes took place, organized by the General Confederation of Labor Unions and public sector unions, along with hundreds of mass marches and occupations of public squares (Della Porta et al., 2017; Kanellopoulos et al. 2017: 108). Public opinion also strongly supported the protests against austerity. The Syriza party was present in 75 percent of major protest events between January 2010 and January 2013 (Kousis 2016: 158). Beyond actively participating in anti-austerity protests, the party consistently stood against privatization and enlisted social movement activists as electoral candidates (Papanikolopoulos and Rongas, 2019).

Syriza's participation in the protest campaigns and strong stance against the neoliberal reforms during the early 2010s catapulted the party from a minor player to the executive branch of government. Indeed, in the first three general parliamentary elections in which Syriza competed between 2004 and 2009, the party averaged about 300,000 votes and 4 percent of seats in the legislative branch. In the two sets of general elections in 2012, after participating as a partner in the massive anti-austerity protest wave since 2010, the party gained 1.06 million votes, and 1.65 million votes respectively, as well as 27 percent of seats in the national parliament. By the 2015 elections, Syriza won the executive branch and 36 percent of seats in the legislature with 2.25 million votes (Della Porta et al., 2017: 43).

Table 7 summarizes the cases of moving from defensive to offensive mobilization against neoliberalism via elections in Latin American and southern Europe. The pathway to electoral success in all of these cases involves an enormous uptick in anti-neoliberal protest, usually long-lasting and coordinated by multiple sectors. Such protest participation provides experience in collective action, interpretative understandings of neoliberal policies, and potential affiliates for anti-neoliberal parties in place of the financial resources of the competing and dominant parties (Almeida et al., 2021). Once an anti-neoliberal party wins a legislative majority or the executive branch of government, the party can slow down neoliberalism and implement alternative models of economic development and social policy.

Table 7 Summary of neoliberal resistance converting to strong electoral parties/outcomes

Country and Years	Type of Neoliberal Policy	Multisectoral Organizations/ Coalitions Promoting Scale Shift	Neoliberal Resistance	Electoral Outcomes
Peru, 1976–8, 2017–21	Bermudez military government implements austerity and cuts social benefits from Velasco regime to receive an IMF loan, 2017 underfunding public education	Regional fronts coordinate 1976–8 anti-austerity wave, National Federation of Education Workers of Peru (FENATE) coordinates 2017 strike	Anti-austerity protests wave in 1977 and 1978 by industrial and state workers, students, and leftist parties. Several general strikes and mass demonstrations, 2017 teachers' strike	Constituent Assembly with left parties in 1978, second largest gain for left parties in Latin American history, LIBRE leftist party grows in strength after 2017 teachers' strike and wins presidency in 2021
Brazil, Workers Party 1982–9	Inflation, foreign debt, multiple structural adjustment programs, and Cruzado anti-inflation programs in the mid-1980s	Central Única dos Trabalhadores (CUT), General Labor Confederation (CGT), Landless Workers Movement (MST)	Workers Party aligned with labor unions, landless peasants, progressive Catholic organizations unleashes a strike wave in 1987 and 1988	Workers' Party (PT), in 1988 PT wins more than 30 city governments, including Sao Paulo. In 1989 presidential elections, PT comes close to winning presidential elections. Institutionalized as second largest party until winning presidential elections in 2002 and holding power through 2018.

Argentina, 1990–95	President Menem massive austerity and privatization program	Central de Trabajadores de Argentina (CTA)	Mass protests, strikes, and marches in the provinces by public sector workers, teachers, and the unemployed	Formation of new party – Patria Grande/FREPASO in 1995. FREPASO wins several seats in parliament, and becomes third largest political party until 2001
Uruguay, 2003–2004	Water privatization	Comisión Nacional en Defensa del Agua y de la Vida	Protests and referendum against water privatization in 2004, Frente Amplio party participates in protests. Referendum on water privatization held simultaneously with 2004 national elections	Frente Amplio party wins presidency and a majority in parliament for first time in 2004. Holds on to power until 2018.
Nicaragua, 1990–2005	Three consecutive neoliberal governments reverse gains of Nicaraguan revolution, hundreds of privatizations, and privatization of agrarian reform lands, water and	Frente Nacional de Trabajadores (FNT), Coordinadora Civil	Massive austerity protests in 1990, anti-neoliberal rural protests in 1995 and 1997, campaign against water privatization, 2000–2003. Massive protests against transportation price increases	Sandinista party remains second largest party in country between 1990 and 2005 through anti-neoliberal advocacy. FSLN wins presidency in 2006 and remains in power.

Table 7 (cont.)

Country and Years	Type of Neoliberal Policy	Multisectoral Organizations/ Coalitions Promoting Scale Shift	Neoliberal Resistance	Electoral Outcomes
	electricity privatization, removal of price controls		in 2005, electricity price hike protests in 2006, 2006 health care campaign against IMF imposed budget and freezes on salaries. Sandinista party activists involved in most campaigns.	
El Salvador, 1999–2007	Health care privatization, free trade, dollarization, water privatization	Labor and Social Alliance (CLS), Foro de la Sociedad Civil, Coordinadora de Organizaciones sociales contra la privatizacion Alianza Ciudadana contra la Privatización, Bloque Popular Social (BPS), Movimiento Popular de Resitencia 12 de Octubre (MPR).	Massive protests against health care privatization between 1999 and 2003 with civil society and FMLN support. Major protests against CAFTA and water privatization between 2004 and 2007.	FMLN gains more seats in parliament than any other party in 2000 and 2003 immediately after supporting campaigns against health care privatization. The FMLN doubles its vote in presidential elections between 1999 and 2004. Wins presidency in 2009 and remains in power until 2019.

Bolivia, 1999–2005	Water and Natural Gas privatizations, regressive taxation	Confederación Sindical Única de Trabajadores Campesinos de Bolivia (CSUTCB), Estado Mayor del Pueblo	Rural and indigenous social movements build links with urban movements and form new political parties. Launch two massive and national-level campaigns over government's neoliberal natural gas extraction and export policies.	MIP and MAS parties grow in strength after protest campaigns. MAS wins presidential elections in 2005 and remains in power until 2019, wins presidency and majority in parliament again in 2021
Mexico, 2017	Deregulation of PEMEX/ Energy Sector Reform, national oil industry	Transportation workers, labor unions, civil society	Massive protests in 2017 against price increases and state petroleum de-regulation (gasolinazo).	Morena party established in 2014, advocates against PEMEX deregulation. Wins presidency and majorities in congress and senate in 2018 elections
Paraguay, 1999–2005	Privatization of Public Industries and Basic Infrastructure	Frente Nacional de Defensa de Bienes Públicas y la Soberanía	Massive protests campaigns against privatization, rural sector participates in large numbers	Left-leaning Catholic Bishop, Fernando Lugo wins presidency in 2008 with Patriotic Alliance for Change Party, breaks up 175-year-old two-party system

Table 7 (cont.)

Country and Years	Type of Neoliberal Policy	Multisectoral Organizations/ Coalitions Promoting Scale Shift	Neoliberal Resistance	Electoral Outcomes
Chile, 2009–21	Privatization of public education, privatization of pensions, rising transportation and health care fees	Confederación de Estudiantes de Chile (CONFECH), Central Unico de Trabajadores (CUT)	Massive student protests between 2009 and 2012. Unprecedented national uprising in October and November against transportation price increases and other neoliberal policies	Frente Amplio Party formed in 2013, wins greater representation in each national election in parliament. Leftist parties and candidates perform well in 2021 constituent assembly elections forced by 2019 uprising. Frente Amplio wins presidency in 2021
Guatemala, 2005–18	CAFTA, power privatization	Frente Nacional de Lucha (FNL)	Several national level protest campaigns against energy and power privatization and electricity prices, protests against CAFTA	New rural and indigenous party formed in 2018 that originates in peasant resistance to neoliberalism. Wins more than 400,000 votes in 2019 presidential elections, most by a left party in post peace Guatemala.

Ecuador, late 1990s and early 2000s	Land and water privatization (1994). Privatization of social security, structural adjustment, price increase (1997–2002). Free Trade (2004–2006)	Coordinadora de los movimientos sociales (CMS), Ecuador Decide	Massive national uprisings against privatizations in 1994, referendum against several privatizations in 1995, other national campaigns against structural adjustment and prices increases between 1997 and 2002. Focused protest campaigns against FTAA and US-Ecuador free trade between 2004 and 2006	Establishment of Pachakutik indigenous and anti-neoliberal party from social movements in 1994. Beginning 1996, the party wins local governments and representation in the national legislature. New anti-neoliberal party formed in 2006, Alianza País and wins presidential elections in 2006 and remains in power until 2019.
Colombia, 2002–2005	Protests against privatization		Protests against social security and other privatizations	Polo Democratico party forms in 2005 as a fusion of parties. Wins Bogota and representation in congress in 2006. Larger split off anti-neoliberal party forms in 2011, Colombia Humana comes in second place in 2018 presidential elections, and won in 2022 as part of the Pacto Histórico coalition following anti-neoliberal protests in 2019 and 2021.

Table 7 (cont.)

Country and Years	Type of Neoliberal Policy	Multisectoral Organizations/ Coalitions Promoting Scale Shift	Neoliberal Resistance	Electoral Outcomes
Honduras, 2000–2021	Structural adjustment, water privatization, CAFTA, special economic zones, health and education privatization		Multisectoral resistance with national days of protest between 2000 and 2008 against water privatization and CAFTA. Resistance to military coup that installs a more pro-neoliberal government between 2009 and 2012. Massive resistance to education and health care privatization in 2019	LIBRE party formed in 2013, comes in second place in 2013 presidential elections and breaks up one hundred-year-old two-party system. Likely won 2017 presidential elections and will likely win 2021 elections. LIBRE emerges out of the anti-neoliberal protest movements. LIBRE wins 2021 Presidential Elections, most plurality of parliamentary seats, and mayorships of major cities.
Venezuela, 1989–97	Several major austerity programs, privatizations, and IMF agreements	CTV, public sector unions	More than 5,000 protests in years following 1999 Caracazo anti-neoliberal uprising. Major wave of strikes and protests in 1996	Small left parties and factions such as Causa R, MAS, and Movimiento Bolivarano Revolucionario built power during austerity protests

			and 1997 following 1996 IMF agreement to raise prices on consumer goods and privatize several industries	during the 1990s until forming a coalition party – MVR – that wins presidential elections at the end of 1988.
Spain, 2009–13	European sovereign debt crisis, Zapatero Austerity Program	15-M Network	General strike in 2009, Indignado anti-austerity protests begin on May 15, 2011, protests and occupations of plazas continue through early 2010s	Formation of new left political party, PODEMOS in 2014. PODEMOS wins seats in European parliament, national legislature and representation in several major cities and regional governments. PODEMOS leaders emerge from May 15 movement
Greece, 2009–15	Foreign debt crisis, TROIKA MOU austerity programs	Direct Democracy Now!, The General Confederation of Greek Workers (GSEE), All Workers; Militant Front, Supreme Administration of Unions of Public Sector Workers	Massive protests, occupation of public squares, general strikes, small left Syriza political party present in most major protest events.	Syriza wins five times more votes in 2012 elections than previous contests and 27% of seats in the legislature. Wins the presidency in 2015 elections.

4 The Future of Neoliberalism and Alternatives

This book offers a global, but not exhaustive, perspective on collective resistance to neoliberalism. Often, there is some historical amnesia about the origins of resistance in the 1970s, as well as an overemphasis in certain world regions, especially Europe since the 2008 Great Recession. The current phase of market fundamentalism continues as a long-term process and appears not to be receding into a post-neoliberal era. Indeed, it is projected that by 2025, 78 percent of people on the planet (6.3 billion) will be living under governments with strict economic austerity measures (Ortiz and Cummins, 2021). By understanding different national contexts across continents, we can make comparisons and learn about the conditions that lead to successful mobilizations and alternatives.

One dimension that scholarship on social movements often misses is the repressive side of neoliberalism for the vulnerable populations that are increasingly excluded from a market-driven economy (including within democratic states). At times, in environments characterized by unemployment, poverty, structural racism, mass incarceration, and over-policing, it becomes difficult to form and sustain large-scale resistance (Cobbina, 2019). Such situations should not be interpreted as compliance with the neoliberal status quo, but a result of repression of potential mass dissent (De Leon and Clarno, 2020; Robinson, 2020). Such extreme conditions may also lead to everyday or covert forms of resistance.

Rightwing Attributions

Another key issue involves the diagnostic framing of the hardships, losses, and trauma associated with neoliberalism. Diagnostic framing has two components: defining the problem and attributing blame (Snow and Corrigal-Brown, 2005; Snow and Benford, 1988). The attribution issue appears fundamental to understanding if opposition to neoliberalism will take a progressive or rightist trajectory. Collective attribution for economic stress acts as a recurring theme in historical sociology, and especially in the choices between socialism, centrist liberalism, or fascism during the Great Depression in the 1930s (Chase-Dunn and Almeida, 2020; Mann, 2012b). As with prior economic formations that generate material hardships, neoliberalism tends to cause both an upswing in rightist and progressive movements as a response to growing inequality and material grievances. In the short term, a specific austerity measure such as privatization or a welfare state cutback tends to produce progressive mobilization that attributes blame to state actors and policymakers. This general pattern is found throughout the world.

Longer-term impacts of neoliberalism since the late 1970s, however, may produce multiple attributions beyond the state and economic structures generating problems of growing inequality, job loss, and downward mobility

(Edelman, 2021). This study has emphasized left-leaning resistance to market fundamentalism. There is a growing body of literature that emphasizes the rise of rightist movements of different persuasions in response to market reforms (Berezin, 2009). This literature tends to emphasize longer-term trends associated with neoliberalism, such as mass unemployment, deindustrialization, and labor market precarity (McVeigh and Estep, 2019; Standing, 2011), as opposed to shorter-term austerity measures. Even in the same world region, Borbáth and Hutter (2021) found that in Eastern Europe right-wing parties tended to mobilize in the street around conservative cultural issues, while in southern Europe left-wing parties more likely mobilized over economic grievances during the years of the Great Recession.

The challenge remains in the contemporary period. When progressive forces fail to sustain mobilization against market reforms or are unable to go on the offensive via electoral politics, the void can be filled by right-wing movements and governments. Rightist activists and leaders will attempt to appropriate the diagnostic framing process in terms of placing attributions for economic problems on vulnerable groups such as on women, ethnic/racial minorities and immigrants – creating a demagogic and artificial form of threat (Almeida and Van Dyke, 2014). This adds another front of struggle for the anti-neoliberal resistance, to counter the xenophobic, inflammatory, and racist appeals of right-wing authoritarian populism (Snow and Bernatzky, 2018). Furthermore, although political and economic elites inaccurately conflated neoliberalism with democracy and democratization from the 1980s to the 2000s, economic and political liberalization are increasingly decoupled.

A newer form of authoritarian neoliberalism can be observed in a wide range of states, including Nicaragua, the United States, India, Brazil, China, Iran, the Philippines, Poland, Russia, Hungary, Cameroon, Gabon, and Kazakhstan. Indeed, the period from 2016 to 2020 finds more countries moving in an authoritarian direction than a democratic direction – the most since the third wave of global democracy in the 1970s (Markoff, 2015; IDEA, 2021). Moreover, one-quarter of the world's population lives in de-democratizing countries while two-thirds of the globe live in authoritarian or de-democratizing nations (IDEA, 2021). This may push anti-neoliberal popular resistance away from elections (as the electoral arena shuts down) with a renewed focus on extra-parliamentary repertoires and potential radicalization.

Alternatives

The present work focused on mobilized resistance to market fundamentalism. An equally valuable line of research beyond the scope of this study explores the policy alternatives to neoliberalism and potential projects that may be achieved in the short term. Even as major transnational movements such as Jubilee Africa and the World Social Forum call for cancellation of the foreign debt in the global South (Bond, 2006), nation states are attempting to address the social damage wrought by a globalized market society. While the global political economy continues to be dominated by a framework of market fundamentalism (even after the Great Recession and global coronavirus pandemic), states and social movements across the globe have ushered in alternative projects that run counter to pure market principles in an attempt to protect large segments of society from social and economic harms. The alternative social institutions and projects range from social solidarity clinics and pharmacies in Greece, to the worker recuperated factories in Argentina (Roussos and Malamidis, 2021; Sobering and Lapegna, 2021).

One major success story involves the *Bolsa Familia* Program in Brazil initiated by the Workers' Party (PT) discussed in Section 3. The program aimed to address one of the most extreme national cases of economic and social inequality in the world. The initiative began in 2003 (immediately after the PT won the presidency). *Bolsa Familia* provided a basic income to an estimated 46 million people in Brazil, about one in four families. It has reduced poverty by double digits, as well as narrowed inequality (Harris and Scully, 2015). Recipients must enroll their children in schools, receive vaccinations, and are offered other social services such as job training workshops. The program has lasted for two decades since inception, operates in more than 5,000 municipal districts, and serves as a model for other initiatives. For instance, city governments in the global North have begun to experiment with similar policies, such as a minimum income program for populations in need in the US cities of Stockton, Los Angeles, and Chicago.

Harris and Scully (2015) have also documented a tremendous rise in social assistance programs similar to *Bolsa Familia* across the global South since the 1990s, including the National Rural Employment Guarantee Act (NREGA) in India, the Minimum Livelihood Guarantee in China, and the Child Support Grant in South Africa. They perceive such programs as a progressive Polanyian countermovement to the deepening of global neoliberalism. Indeed, before 1990, there were less than twenty flagship social assistance programs (major cash transfer/basic income redistribution programs for the poor) in low- and medium-income countries. By 2012, there were at least 150 massive social assistance programs in operation across the global South, benefitting at minimum, one billion people (Harris and Scully, 2015). More contemporary initiatives include Togo's new Novissi cash transfer program and Honduras's new electricity and fuel subsidies for the poor with the LIBRE government.

In another alternative policy example, the Bolivian government under the newly installed MAS party, implemented the first universal pension program in

Latin America in late 2007 – *Renta Dignidad*. The progressive legislation overcame the dominant private pension programs in place by taxing foreign oil and gas extraction. The pension policy was bolstered by the support of neighborhood-based associations that took to the streets to ensure the passage of the legislation when right-wing legislators began to resist (Anria and Niedzwiecki, 2016).

Another major and locally based alternative to neoliberalism is found in participatory budgeting programs (Baiocchi and Ganuza, 2014), whereby local populations are empowered to participate in the distribution of municipal and regional expenditures in the global North and South, with a goal of investing in vulnerable populations and social programs most in need. Already by 2010, a reported 1,500 municipalities around the world enacted participatory budgeting assemblies (Miller et al., 2019), including in the California cities of Fresno and Merced. Finally, out of the austerity protests in Spain in the early 2010s, and specifically from the collective efforts of the Plataforma de Afectados por la Hipoteca (PAH) movement, local government in Barcelona and the national government have enacted progressive housing policies. The innovative policies include a moratorium on paying mortgage debt, subsidies for low-income renters, prohibition of privatization of public housing, and taxing landlords for vacant housing properties (Flesher Fominaya, 2015; Martínez, 2019).

Growing Environmental Crises

The crisis of climate change did not begin with neoliberalism. Global warming has roots in the industrial revolution and earlier forms of capitalism and authoritarian state socialism with the unprecedented levels of carbon dioxide released into the atmosphere over the past 150 years. Nonetheless, neoliberalism is the dominant economic formation of our time, and with its deregulatory and hyper-growth emphases, will likely continue to accelerate planetary heating. IMF and World Bank structural adjustment agreements often explicitly call for greater foreign investment in mining, forest, and energy resources (Bebbington and Bury, 2013). The terrain of conflict will likely begin to shift from largely economic struggles over austerity and convert into protracted confrontations to protect the environment and slow down climate change. Some contend that this shift has already taken place with the global economic justice movement spilling over into the transnational climate movement (Hadden, 2014). The deepening ecological crisis of climate change may force more reforms or complete alternatives to the current dominance of neoliberalism. In the short and medium term, activists have begun to march into local institutions and develop clean energy programs to reduce the use of fossil fuels and the release of greenhouse gases such as California's Community Choice

Aggregation program and Spain's Som Energia. In the long term, the "Green New Deals" and the battle to transition to a green economy have just commenced.

As outlined in Section 1, neoliberalism is also a compelling belief system. For a major shift to emerge, a change in the mentalities of individualism and consumerism would also need to occur. One ecological alternative to market fundamentalism gaining traction in the ideational sphere derives from South America, referred to as "Buen Vivir." The Buen Vivir or Sumak Kawsay (good living or living well in Quechua) is a central element within the philosophy of life held by indigenous communities (Acosta, 2012: 196). It questions the ethics of "living better," if this means unlimited economic growth, permanent competition, and results in ecological unsustainability (Acosta, 2012: 195). With Buen Vivir, there is no linear process of life in the sense of a former and subsequent state, as in the dichotomous representation of "underdeveloped" vs "developed" nations. This holistic point of view also implies a harmonious and respectful relationship with the Pachamama (Our Mother Earth).

In its formal expression, the Buen Vivir or Vivir Bien was incorporated into the new Constitutions of Ecuador (2008) and Bolivia (2009) after anti-neoliberal protests campaigns converted into election victories (Silva, 2015). In both cases, Buen Vivir appears as a key element to rethink what we understand as "development" (Gudynas, 2011). For instance, the legal recognition of nature as a subject of rights in the Ecuadorean Constitution was accompanied by mandates of decommodification of natural resources and the promotion of food sovereignty. Also, a solidarity economy was incorporated as a set of relations of production, exchange, and cooperation that promotes sufficiency and quality, underpinned by reciprocity. Yet, the 2022 Paro Nacional led by the indigenous movement in Ecuador still demands fair prices of agricultural products, to stop the expansion of oil extraction, and reparations for environmental impacts.

Beyond the Ecuadorean experience, local projects and networks of a social and solidarity economy (SSE) exist across the world, such as the Red de Redes de Economía Alternativa y Solidaria (REAS) in Spain, and Fórum Brasileiro de Economia Solidária (FBES) in Brazil. The global Covid pandemic has perhaps hastened the process of reconsidering the pace and habits of neoliberalism, but the ongoing diagnostic dispute of causal attribution and blame for health, environmental, and economic crises continues with enormous consequences for humanity and nature.

References

Abouharb, M. R. and Cingranelli, D. (2007). *Human Rights and Structural Adjustment*. Cambridge: Cambridge University Press.

Abouharb, M. R., Cingranelli, D. L. and Filippov, M. (2015). "Do Non-Human Rights Regimes Undermine the Achievement of Economic and Social Rights?" In L. Haglund and R. Stryker, eds., *Closing the Rights Gap: From Human Rights to Social Transformation*. 1st ed. Berkeley: University of California Press, pp. 29–48.

Abouharb, M. R. and Fordham, B. O. (2020). "Trade and Strike Activity in the Postwar United States." *Social Sciences*, 9(11), 1–25.

Acosta, A. (2012). "The *Buen Vivir*: An Opportunity to Imagine Another World." In D. D. Bartelt, ed., *Inside a Champion: An Analysis of the Brazilian Development Model*. Berlin: Heinrich Boll Foundation, pp. 192–210.

Alexander, M. (2010). *The New Jim Crow: Mass Incarceration in the Age of Colorblindness*. New York: New Press.

Almeida, P. (2006). "Social Movement Unionism, Social Movement Partyism, and Policy Outcomes." In H. Johnston and P. Almeida, eds., *Latin American Social Movements: Globalization, Democratization, and Transnational Networks*. Lanham, MD: Rowman and Littlefield, pp. 57–76.

Almeida, P. (2007). "Defensive Mobilization: Popular Movements Against Economic Adjustment Policies in Latin America." *Latin American Perspectives*, 34(3), 123–139.

Almeida, P. (2008). "The Sequencing of Success: Organizing Templates and Neoliberal Policy Outcomes." *Mobilization* 13(2), 165–187.

Almeida, P. (2010). "Social Movement Partyism: Collective Action and Oppositional Political Parties." In N. Van Dyke and H. McCammon, eds., *Strategic Alliances: Coalition Building and Social Movements*. Minneapolis: University of Minnesota Press, pp. 170–196.

Almeida, P. (2012). "Subnational Opposition to Globalization." *Social Forces*, 90(4), 1051–1072.

Almeida, P. (2014). *Mobilizing Democracy: Globalization and Citizen Protest*. Baltimore, MD: Johns Hopkins University Press.

Almeida, P. (2015). "Unintended Consequences of State-led Development: A Theory of Collective Opposition to Neoliberalism." *Sociology of Development*, 1(2), 259–276.

Almeida, P. (2019a). "The Role of Threat in Collective Action." In D. Snow, S. Soule, H. Kriesi and H. McCammon, eds., *The Wiley Blackwell Companion to Social Movements*. Oxford: Wiley Blackwell, pp. 43–62.

Almeida, P. (2019b). *Social Movements: The Structure of Collective Mobilization*. Oakland: University of California Press.

Almeida, P. and Chase-Dunn, C. (2018). "Globalization and Social Movements." *Annual Review of Sociology*, 44(1), 189–211.

Almeida, P. et al. (2021). "Protest Waves and Social Movement Fields: The Micro Foundations of Campaigning for Subaltern Political Parties." *Social Problems*, 68(4), 831–851.

Almeida, P. and Lichbach, M. (2003). "To The Internet, From The Internet: Comparative Media Coverage Of Transnational Protests." *Mobilization: An International Quarterly*, 8(3), 249–272.

Almeida, P. and Pérez Martín, A. (2021). "Economic Globalization and Social Movements in Latin America." In X. Bada and L. Rivera, eds., *The Oxford Handbook of the Sociology of Latin America*. Oxford: Oxford University Press, pp. 391–414.

Almeida, P. and Van Dyke, N. (2014). "Social Movement Partyism and the Tea Party's Rapid Mobilization." In N. Van Dyke and D. Meyer, eds., *Understanding the Tea Party Movement*. London: Ashgate, pp. 55–72.

Alvarado Alcázar, A. et al. (2020). "Protesta y Covid-19 en Costa Rica: Informe Marzo-Julio 2020." *Protestas: Base de Datos de Acciones Colectivas*. San José: IIS, Universidad de Costa Rica.

Alvarado Alcázar, A. and Martínez Sánchez, G. (2018). *Protestas de Septiembre, Octubre, Noviembre de 2018*. San José: IIS, Universidad de Costa Rica.

Alvarado Alcázar, A. and Martínez Sánchez, G. (2021). *Protestas: Base de Datos de Acciones Colectivas*. San José: IIS, Universidad de Costa Rica.

Álvarez-Rivadulla, M. (2017). *Squatters and the Politics of Marginality in Uruguay*. Cham: Palgrave/Macmillan.

Amenta, E., Andrews, K. and Caren, N. (2018). "The Political Institutions, Processes, and Outcomes Movements Seek to Influence." In D. Snow, S. Soule, H. Kriesi and H. McCammon, eds., *The Wiley Blackwell Companion to Social Movements*. Hoboken, NJ: John Wiley & Sons, pp. 447–465.

Andrews, A. (2010). "Constructing Mutuality: The Zapatistas' Transformation of Transnational Activist Power Dynamics." *Latin American Politics and Society*, 52(1), 89–120.

Andrews, A. (2011). "How Activists 'Take Zapatismo Home': South-to-North Dynamics in Transnational Social Movements." *Latin American Perspectives*, 38(1), 138–152.

Anner, M. and Evans, P. (2004). "Building Bridges Across a Double Divide: Alliances between US and Latin American Labour and NGOs." *Development in Practice*, 14(1–2), 34–47.

Anria, S. (2018). *When Movements Become Parties: The Bolivian MAS in Comparative Perspective*. Cambridge: Cambridge University Press.

Anria, S. and Niedzwiecki, S. (2016). "Social Movements and Social Policy: the Bolivian Renta Dignidad." *Studies in Comparative International Development*, 51(3), 308–327.

Arce, M. (2008). "The Repoliticization of Collective Action After Neoliberalism in Peru." *Latin American Politics and Society*, 50(3), 37–62.

Arce, M. and Mangonnet, J. (2013). "Competitiveness, Partisanship, and Subnational Protest in Argentina." *Comparative Political Studies*, 46(8), 895–919.

Archila Neira, M. (2021). *A parar para avanzar*. http://jlacs-travesia.online/en/2021/05/30/a-parar-para-avanzar/.

Auyero, J. (2004). "The Moral Politics of Argentine Crowds." *Mobilization*, 9 (3), 311–326.

Auyero, J., Bourgois, P. and Scheper-Hughes, N. (eds.) (2015). *Violence at the Urban Margins*. New York: Oxford University Press.

Auyero, J. and Moran, T. (2007). "The Dynamics of Collective Violence: Dissecting Food Riots in Contemporary Argentina." *Social Forces*, 85(3), 1341–1367.

Auyero, J. and Swistun, D. (2009). *Flammable: Environmental Suffering in an Argentine Shantytown*. Oxford: Oxford University Press.

Ayres, J. (1998). *Defying Conventional Wisdom: Political Movements and Popular Attention Against North American Free Trade*. Toronto: University of Toronto Press.

Babb, S., and Kentikelenis, A. (2021). "Markets Everywhere: The Washington Consensus and the Sociology of Global Institutional Change." *Annual Review of Sociology*, 47(1), 521–541.

Baiocchi, G. and Ganuza, E. (2014). "Participatory Budgeting As If Emancipation Mattered." *Politics & Society*, 42(1), 29–50.

Baker, A. (2009). *The Market and the Masses*. Cambridge: Cambridge University Press.

Barbosa Cano, F. and González Arévalo, A. (1984). "Expresiones de la Conflictividad Social en la Crisis. El Paro Cívico Nacional." *Momento Económico*, 5, 3–5.

Barlow, M. and Clarke, T. (2002). *Blue Gold: The Battle Against Corporate Theft of the World's Water*. London: Routledge.

Bayat, A. (2010). *Life as Politics: How Ordinary People Change the Middle East*. Stanford, CA: Stanford University Press.

Bebbington, A. and Bury, J. (eds.) (2013). *Subterranean Struggles: New Dynamics of Mining, Oil, and Gas in Latin America*. Austin: University of Texas Press.

Becker, M. (2011). *Pachakutik!: Indigenous Movements and Electoral Politics in Ecuador*. Lanham, MD: Rowman and Littlefield.

Beluche, O. (1994). *Diez años de luchas políticas y sociales en Panamá, 1980–1990*. Panama: CELA.

Berezin, M. (2009). *Illiberal Politics in Neoliberal Times: Culture, Security and Populism in the New Europe*. Cambridge: Cambridge University Press.

Bergstrand, K. (2014). "The Mobilizing Power of Grievances: Applying Loss Aversion and Omission Bias to Social Movements." *Mobilization: An International Quarterly*, 19(2), 123–142.

Bernburg, J. (2015). "Economic Crisis and Popular Protest in Iceland, January 2009: The Role of Perceived Economic Loss and Political Attitudes in Protest Participation and Support." *Mobilization*, 20(2), 231–252.

Bidegain, G. and Tricot, V. (2017). "Political Opportunity Structure, Social Movements, and Malaise in Representation in Uruguay, 1985–2014." In A. Joignant, M. Morales and C. Fuentes, eds., *Malaise in Representation in Latin American Countries: Chile, Argentina, and Uruguay*. New York: Springer, pp. 139–160.

Bieler, A. and Jordan, J. (2018). "Commodification and 'the Commons': The Politics of Privatising Public Water in Greece and Portugal during the Eurozone Crisis." *European Journal of International Relations*, 24(4), 934–957.

Blanc, E. (2021). "How Digitized Strategy Impacts Movement Outcomes: Social Media, Mobilizing, and Organizing in the 2018 Teachers' Strikes." *Politics & Society*. https://doi.org/10.1177/00323292211039953.

Bockman, J. (2013). "Neoliberalism." *Contexts*, 12(3), 14–15.

Bockman, J. and Eyal, G. (2002). "Eastern Europe as a Laboratory for Economic Knowledge: The Transnational Roots of Neoliberalism." *American Journal of Sociology*, 108(2), 310–352.

Bojar, A., Gessler, T., Hutter, S., and Kriesi, H. (Eds.). (2021). *Contentious episodes in the age of austerity: studying the dynamics of government–challenger interactions*. Cambridge, NY: Cambridge University Press.

Bond, P. (2006). *Looting Africa: The Economics of Exploitation*. Scottsville: University of KwaZulu-Natal Press.

Borbáth, E. and Hutter, S. (2021). "Protesting Parties in Europe: A Comparative Analysis." *Party Politics*, 27(5), 896–908.

Brenner, N., Peck, J. and Theodore, N. (2010). "After Neoliberalization?" *Globalizations*, 7(3), 327–345.

Brown, W. (2015). *Undoing the Demos: Neoliberalism's Stealth Revolution*. New York: Zone Books.

Bruhn, K. (2008). *Urban Protest in Mexico and Brazil*. Cambridge: Cambridge University Press.

Burridge, D. and Markoff, J. (2022). "Social Movements and Globalization in Latin America." In F. Rossi, ed., *Oxford Handbook of Latin American Social Movements*. Oxford: Oxford University Press.

Burstein, P., Einwohner, R. and Hollander, J. (1995) "The Success of Political Movements: A Bargaining Perspective." In J. C. Jenkins, ed., *The Politics of Social Protest: Comparative Perspectives on States and Social Movements*. Minneapolis: University of Minnesota Press, pp. 275–295.

Cadena-Roa, J. (1988). "Las Demandas de La Sociedad Civil, Los Partidos Políticos, y Las Respuestas Del Sistema." In P. Gonzalez Casanovas and J. Cadena Roa, eds., *Primer informe sobre la democracia: México 1988*. Mexico City: Siglo XXI Editores, pp. 285–327.

Cadena-Roa, J. and Alonso, J. (2004). *Las organizaciones civiles mexicanas hoy*. Mexico City: UNAM Press.

Canizales, S. (2021). "Work Primacy and the Social Incorporation of Unaccompanied, Undocumented Latinx Youth in the United States." *Social Forces*, soab152.

Castells, M. (2013). *Communication Power*. Oxford, New York: Oxford University Press.

Centeno, M. and Cohen, J. (2012). "The Arc of Neoliberalism." *Annual Review of Sociology*, 38(1), 317–340.

Chase-Dunn, C. and Almeida, P. (2020). *Global Struggles and Social Change: From Prehistory to World Revolution in the Twenty-First Century*. Baltimore, MD: Johns Hopkins University Press.

Chong, A. and López-de-Silanes, F. (2005). "The Truth About Privatization in Latin America." In A. Chong and F. López de-Silanes, eds., *Privatization in Latin America: Myths and Reality*. Palo Alto: Stanford University Press, pp. 1–66.

Claeys, P. and Edelman, M. (2020). "The United Nations Declaration on the Rights of Peasants and Other People Working in Rural Areas." *The Journal of Peasant Studies*, 47(1), 1–68.

Cobbina, J. (2019). *Hands Up, Don't Shoot: Why the Protests in Ferguson and Baltimore Matter, and How They Changed America*. New York: New York University Press.

Cordero, A. (in press). "Protests against the 2018 Fiscal Reform in Costa Rica." In D. Snow, D. Della Porta, and D. McAdam, eds., *Wiley Blackwell Encyclopedia of Social and Political Movements*. Oxford: Wiley Blackwell.

Cordero, A., Barahona, M. and Sibaja, P. (2020). *Protesta y Movilización Social En Tiempos de Pandemia: Algunas Tendencias, Características y Preguntas*. San José, CR: FLACSO.

Curran, M., Schwarz, E. and Chase-Dunn, C. (2015). "The Occupy Movement in California." In T. A. Comer, ed., *What Comes After Occupy?: The Regional Politics of Resistance*. Cambridge: Cambridge Scholars Publishing, pp. 190–207.

Davis, A. (2003). *Are Prisons Obsolete?* New York: Seven Stories Press.

De Giorgi, A. (2017). "Back to Nothing: Prisoner Reentry and Neoliberal Neglect." *Social Justice*, 44(1), 83–120.

De Leon, C. and Clarno, A. (2020). "Power." In T. Janoski, C. de Leon, J. Misra and I. Martin, eds., *The New Handbook of Political Sociology*. Cambridge: Cambridge University Press, pp. 35–52.

De Sousa Santos, B. (2004). "The World Social Forum: Toward a Counter-Hegemonic Globalisation (Part II)." In J. Sen and P. Waterman, eds., *World Social Forum: Challenging Empires*. New Delhi: The Viveka Foundation, pp. 336–343.

Della Porta, D. (2015). *Social Movements in Times of Austerity: Bringing Capitalism Back into Protest Analysis*. Malden, MA: Polity Press.

Della Porta, D. (2017). "Political Economy and Social Movement Studies: The Class Basis of Anti-Austerity Protests." *Anthropological Theory*, 17(4), 453–473.

Della Porta, D., Fernández, J., Kouki, H. and Mosca, L. (2017). *Movement Parties Against Austerity*. Cambridge: Polity Press.

Díaz Alba, C. L. (2021). "The World March of Women: Popular Feminisms, Transnational Struggles." *Latin American Perspectives*, 48(5), 96–112.

Dicken, P. (2015). *Global Shift: Seventh Edition: Mapping the Changing Contours of the World Economy*. New York: Guilford Press.

Donoso, S. and Somma, N. (2021). "The Student Movement in Chile: Reshaping Both the Contents and Terms of Politics." In J. Bessant, A. Mejías Mesinas and S. Pickard, eds., *When Students Protest*. Lanham, MD: Rowman & Littlefield.

Dufour, P. and Giraud, I. (2007). "The Continuity of Transnational Solidarities in the World March of Women, 2000 and 2005: A Collective Identity-Building Approach." *Mobilization: An International Quarterly*, 12(3), 307–322.

Edelman, M. (1999). *Peasants Against Globalization: Rural Social Movements in Costa Rica*. Stanford, CA: Stanford University Press.

Edelman, M. (2021). "Hollowed out Heartland, USA: How Capital Sacrificed Communities and Paved the Way for Authoritarian Populism." *Journal of Rural Studies*, 82, 505–517.

Evans, P. and Sewell, W. (2013). "The Neoliberal Era: Ideology, Politics and Social Effects." In Peter A. Hall and M. Lamont, eds., *Social Resilience in the Neoliberal Era*. Cambridge, MA: Cambridge University Press, pp. 35–68.

Fernandez, L. (2008). *Policing Dissent: Social Control and the Anti-Globalization Movement*. New Brunswick, NJ: Rutgers University Press.

Fiedlschuster, M. (2018). *Globalization, EU Democracy Assistance and the World Social Forum: Concepts and Practices of Democracy*. Cham: Palgrave Macmillan.

Fischer, D. (2021). "Unintended but Consequential? The NoG20 Protests in Hamburg and the Introduction of a Police Identification Statute." *Partecipazione e Conflitto*, 14(3), 1076–1101.

Flesher Fominaya, C. (2015). "Redefining the Crisis/Redefining Democracy: Mobilising for the Right to Housing in Spain's PAH Movement." *South European Society and Politics*, 20(4), 465–485.

Flesher Fominaya, C. (2017). "European Anti-austerity and Pro-democracy Protests in the Wake of the Global Financial Crisis." *Social Movement Studies*, 16(1), 1–20.

Flesher Fominaya, C. (2020a). *Social Movements in a Globalized World*. London: McMillan.

Flesher Fominaya, C. (2020b). *Democracy Reloaded: Inside Spain's Political Laboratory from 15-M to Podemos*. Oxford: Oxford University Press.

Fligstein, N. and McAdam, D. (2012). *A Theory of Fields*. Oxford: Oxford University Press.

Flores, E. O. (2018). *Jesus Saved an Ex-Con: Political Activism and Redemption after Incarceration*. New York: New York University Press.

Fourcade-Gourinchas, M. and Babb, S. (2002). "The Rebirth of the Liberal Creed: Paths to Neoliberalism in Four Countries." *American Journal of Sociology*, 108(3), 533–579.

Gamson, W. (1975). *The Strategy of Social Protest*. Homewood, IL: Dorsey Press.

Ganz, M. (2009). *Why David Sometimes Wins: Leadership, Organization, and Strategy in the California Farm Worker Movement*. Oxford: Oxford University Press.

Garland Mahler, A. (2018). *From the Tricontinental to the Global South. Race, Radicalism, and Transnational Solidarity*. Durham, NC: Duke University Press.

Gates, L. (2010). *Electing Chávez: The Business of Anti-neoliberal Politics in Venezuela*. Pittsburgh, PA: University of Pittsburgh Press.

Gessler, T. and Schulte-Cloos, J. (2020). "The Return of the Economy? Issue Contention in the Protest Arena." In H. Kriesi, J. Lorenzini, B. Wüest and S. Häusermann, eds., *Contention in Times of Crisis: Recession and Political Protest in Thirty European Countries*. Cambridge: Cambridge University Press, pp. 128–146.

Gillham, P., Lindstedt, N., Edwards, B. and Johnson, E. (2019). "The Mobilizing Effects of Economic Threats and Resources on the Formation of Local Occupy Wall Street Protest Groups in 2011." *Sociological Perspectives*, 62(4), 433–454.

Gilmore, R. (2007). *Golden Gulag: Prisons, Surplus, Crisis, and Opposition in Globalizing California*. Berkeley: University of California Press.

Godinez Galay, F. and Binder, I. (2021). "Las cámaras que nos pusiste van a volver: Redes sociales y denuncia de los abusos de las fuerzas de seguridad en las protestas de Chile 2019–2020." *Revista de la Asociación Española de Investigación de la Comunicación*, 8(15), 357–387.

Golash-Boza, T. (2015). *Deported: Immigrant Policing, Disposable Labor and Global Capitalism*. New York: New York University Press.

Goldstone, J. and Tilly, C. (2001). "Threat (and opportunity): Popular Action and State Response in the Dynamics of Contentious Action." In C. Tilly et al., eds., *Silence and Voice in the Study of Contentious Politics*. Cambridge: Cambridge University Press, pp. 179–194.

González Rivas, M. and Schroering, C. (2021). "Pittsburgh's Translocal Social Movement: A Case of the New Public Water." *Utilities Policy*, 71, 101230.

Gudynas, E. (2011). "Buen vivir: Germinando alternativas al desarrollo." *America Latina en Movimiento ALAI*, 462, 1–20.

Haber, P. (2006). *Power from Experience: Urban Popular Movements in Late Twentieth-Century Mexico*. State College: Penn State University Press.

Hadden, J. (2014). "Explaining Variation in Transnational Climate Change Activism: The Role of Inter-Movement Spillover." *Global Environmental Politics*, 14(2), 7–25.

Hadden, J. and Tarrow, S. (2007). "Spillover or Spillout? The Global Justice Movement in the United States After 9/11." *Mobilization*, 12(4), 359–376.

Haglund, L. (2010). *Limiting Resources: Market-Led Reform and the Transformation of Public Goods*. State College: Penn State University Press.

Han, H., McKenna, E. and Oyakawa, M. (2021). *Prisms of the People: Power & Organizing in Twenty-First Century America*. Chicago, IL: University of Chicago Press.

Harris, K. and Scully, B. (2015). "A Hidden Counter-Movement? Precarity, Politics, and Social Protection Before and Beyond the Neoliberal Era." *Theory and Society*, 44(5), 415–444.

Harvey, D. (2005). *A Brief History of Neoliberalism*. Oxford: Oxford University Press.

Hutter, S. (2014). "Protest Event Analysis and Its Offspring." In D. Della Porta, ed., *Methodological Practices in Social Movement Research*. Oxford: Oxford University Press, pp. 335–367.

IDEA. (2021). *The Global State of Democracy 2021: Building Resilience in a Pandemic Era*. Stockholm: International Institute for Democracy and Electoral Assistance.

Inclán, M. (2012). "Zapatista and Counter-Zapatista Protests: A test of Movement–Countermovement Dynamics." *Journal of Peace Research*, 49(3), 459–472.

Inclán, M. (2018). *The Zapatista Movement and Mexico's Democratic Transition: Mobilization, Success, and Survival*. New York: Oxford University Press.

Johnston, H. (2005). "Talking the Walk: Speech Acts and Resistance in Authoritarian Regimes." In C. Davenport, H. Johnston and C. Mueller, eds., *Repression and Mobilization*. Minneapolis: University of Minnesota Press, pp. 108–137.

Kadivar, A., Khani, S. and Sotoudeh, A. (2019). "Iran's Protests Are Not Just About Gas Prices." *Foreign Affairs*, December 4.

Kanellopoulos, K., Kostopoulos, K., Papanikolopoulos, D. and Rongas, V. (2017). "Competing Modes of Coordination in the Greek Anti-austerity Campaign, 2010–2012." *Social Movement Studies*, 16(1), 101–118.

Keck, M. (1992). *The Workers' Party and Democratization in Brazil*. New Haven, CT: Yale University Press.

Kentikelenis, A. (2017). "Structural Adjustment and Health: A Conceptual Framework and Evidence on Pathways." *Social Science & Medicine*, (1982)187, 296–305.

Kentikelenis, A. and Babb, S. (2019). "The Making of Neoliberal Globalization: Norm Substitution and the Politics of Clandestine Institutional Change." *American Journal of Sociology*, 124(6), 1720–1762.

Kentikelenis, A., Stubbs, T. and King, L. (2016). "IMF Conditionality and Development Policy Space, 1985–2014." *Review of International Political Economy*, 23(4), 543–582.

Klandermans, B. (1992). "The Social Construction of Protest and Multiorganizational Fields." In C. Mueller and A. Morris, eds., *Frontiers in Social Movement Theory*. New Haven, CT: Yale University Press, pp. 77–103.

Klandermans, B. (1997). *The Social Psychology of Protest*. Oxford: Blackwell.

Koopmans, R. (1999). "The Use of Protest Event Data in Comparative Research: Cross-National Comparability, Sampling Methods, and Robustness." In D. Rucht, R. Koopmans and F. Neidhardt, eds., *Acts of Dissent: New Developments in the Study of Protest*. Lanham, MD: Rowman & Littlefield, pp. 90–110.

Kousis, M. (2016). "The Spatial Dimensions of the Greek Protest Campaign Against the Troika's Memoranda and Austerity, 2010–2013." In M. Ancelovici, P. Dufour and H. Nez, eds., *Street Politics in the Age of Austerity: From Indignados to Occupy*. Amsterdam: University of Amsterdam Press, pp. 147–173.

Kriesi, H. (2020). "Overall Trends of Protest in the Great Recession." In B. Wüest, H. Kriesi, J. Lorenzini and S. Hausermann, eds., *Contention in*

Times of Crisis: Recession and Political Protest in Thirty European Countries. Cambridge: Cambridge University Press, pp. 77–103.

Krippner, G. (2011). *Capitalizing on Crisis: The Political Origins of the Rise of Finance*. Cambridge, MA: Harvard University Press.

Lichbach, M. (2003). "The Anti-Globalization Movement: A New Kind of Protest." In M. Marshall and T. Gurr, eds., *Peace and Conflict*. College Park: Cent. Int. Dev. Confl. Manag., Univ. Md, pp. 39–42.

Lobina, E., Weghmann, V. and Marwa, M. (2019). "Water Justice Will Not Be Televised: Moral Advocacy and the Struggle for Transformative Remunicipalisation in Jakarta." *Water Alternatives*, 12, 725–748.

López Maya, M. (2005). *Del Viernes Negro al Referendo Revocatorio*. Caracas: Alfadil.

López Pardo, G. (1984). "La Construcción de Un Proyecto de Masas: La Asamblea Nacional Obrera, Campesina y Popular." *Momento Económico*, 5, 6–7.

Luna, J. (2007). "Frente Amplio and the Crafting of a Social Democratic Alternative in Uruguay." *Latin American Politics and Society*, 49(4), 1–30.

Mann, M. (2012a). *The Sources of Social Power, Volume 4: Globalizations, 1945–2011*. Cambridge: Cambridge University Press.

Mann, M. (2012b). *The Sources of Social Power, Volume 3: Global Empires, 1890–1945*. Cambridge: Cambridge University Press.

Markoff, J. (1996). *The Abolition of Feudalism: Peasants, Lords, and Legislators in the French Revolution*. State College: Penn State University Press.

Markoff, J. (2015). *Waves of Democracy: Social Movements and Political Change*. London: Routledge.

Markoff, J. and Montecinos, V. (1993). "The Ubiquitous Rise of Economists." *Journal of Public Policy*, 13(1), 37–68.

Martin, A. (2008). "The Institutional Logic of Union Organizing and the Effectiveness of Social Movement Repertoires." *American Journal of Sociology*, 113(4), 1067–1103.

Martin, A. and Dixon, M. (2010). "Changing to Win? Threat, Resistance, and the Role of Unions in Strikes, 1984–2002." *American Journal of Sociology*, 116(1), 93–129.

Martínez, M. (2019). "Bitter Wins or a Long-Distance Race? Social and Political Outcomes of the Spanish Housing Movement." *Housing Studies*, 34(10), 1588–1611.

Marwell, G. and Oliver, P. (1984). "Collective Action Theory and Social Movements Research." *Research in Social Movements, Conflicts, and Change*, 7, 1–27.

McAdam, D. and Tarrow, S. (2010). “Ballots and Barricades: On the Reciprocal Relationship Between Elections and Social Movements.” *Perspectives on Politics*, 8(2), 529–542.

McKenzie, D. and Mookherjee, D. (2005). “Paradox and Perception: Evidence from Four Latin American Countries.” In *Reality Check: The Distributional Impact of Privatization in Developing Countries*. Washington, DC: Center for Global Development, pp. 33–84.

McVeigh, R. and Estep, K. (2019). *The Politics of Losing: Trump, the Klan, and the Mainstreaming of Resentment*. New York: Columbia University Press.

Medina, M. (1999). “El neoliberalismo en Colombia y las alternativas de las luchas sociales 1975–1998.” In M. López Maya, ed., *Lucha popular, democracia, neoliberalismo: protesta popular en América Latina en los años de ajuste*. Caracas: Nueva Sociedad, pp. 111–128.

Meyer, D. (2021). *How Social Movements (Sometimes) Matter*. London: Polity.

Meyer, D. and Staggenborg, S. (1996). “Movements, Countermovements, and the Structure of Political Opportunity.’ *American Journal of Sociology*, 101 (6), 1628–1660.

Miller, S., Hildreth, R. W. and Stewart, L. (2019). “The Modes of Participation: A Revised Frame for Identifying and Analyzing Participatory Budgeting Practices.” *Administration & Society*, 51(8), 1254–1281.

Moody, K. (1997). *Workers in a Lean World: Unions in the International Economy*. London: Verso.

Moreno, M., Amézquita Ochoa, A. and Mejía, A. (2021). “‘Dignidad Para Cambiar El Mundo:. Los Sujetos Del Paro de Octubre de 2019 En Ecuador.” In *Desbordes. Estallidos, sujetos y porvenires en América Latina*. Quito: Fundación Rosa Luxemburgo, pp. 77–116.

Mudge, S. (2018). *Leftism Reinvented. Western Parties from Socialism to Neoliberalism*. Cambridge, MA: Harvard University Press.

Narayanan, S. (2020). “Understanding Farmer Protests in India.” *Academics Stand Against Poverty*, 1(1), 1–8.

O’Connor, J. (1973). *The Fiscal Crisis of the State*. New York: St. Martins.

Ortiz Crespo, S. (2020). “Ecuador: deriva autoritaria y levantamiento indígena y popular.” In F. Ramírez Gallegos, ed., *Octubre y el derecho a la Resistencia: Revuelta popular y neoliberalismo autoritario en Ecuador*. Buenos Aires: CLACSO, pp. 85–110.

Ortiz, I. and Cummins, M. (2021). “Austerity: The New Normal – A Renewed Washington Consensus 2010–24.” *SSRN Electronic Journal*.

Padilla, A. (in press). “Fight for $15 Minimum Wage (U.S.).” In D. Snow, D. Della Porta and D. McAdam, eds., *Wiley Blackwell Encyclopedia of Social and Political Movements*. Oxford: Wiley Blackwell.

Palmtag, T., Rommel, T. and Walter, S. (2020). "International Trade and Public Protest: Evidence from Russian Regions." *International Studies Quarterly*, 64(4), 939–955.

Papanikolopoulos, D. and Rongas, V. (2019). "Movement, Party and Electoral Dynamics: Syriza's Electoral Success as a Movement Effect (2010–2015)." *Greek Political Science Review*, 45, 184–206.

Peck, J. (2010). *Constructions of Neoliberal Reason*. Oxford: Oxford University Press.

Pérez Martín, A. (in press). "Collective Action in Cuba." In D. Snow, D. Della Porta and D. McAdam, eds., *Wiley Blackwell Encyclopedia of Social and Political Social Movements*. Oxford: Wiley Blackwell.

Pérez Martín, A. (2016). *Derecho y movimiento social: una mirada comparativa de la movilización legal como repertorio de la CONAIE en la contienda política por el agua (1994–2001 y 2008–2015)*. Master's Thesis. Quito: FLACSO.

Pérez Martín, A. (2020). *La revolución contra Texaco: 60 años después*. https://oncubanews.com/cuba-ee-uu/la-revolucion-contra-texaco-60-anos-despues/

Pianta, M. and Marchetti, R. (2007). "The Global Justice Movement: The Transnational Dimension." In D. Della Porta, ed., *The Global Justice Movement: A Cross-National and Transnational Perspective*. Boulder, CO: Paradigm, pp. 29–51.

Piketty, T. (2014). *Capital in the Twenty-First Century*. Cambridge, MA: Harvard University Press.

Pinard, M. (2011). *Motivational dimensions in social movements and contentious collective action*. Montreal: McGill-Queen's University Press.

Polanyi, K. (1944). *The Great Transformation: The Political and Economic Origins of Our Time*. Beacon Press.

Prasad, M. (2006). *The Politics of Free Markets: The Rise of Neoliberal Economic Policies in Britain, France, Germany, and the United States*. Chicago, IL: University of Chicago Press.

Prechel, H. and Berkowitz, L. (2020). "Conflict Theories in Political Sociology: Class, Power, Inequality, and the Historical Transition to Financialization." In T. Janoski, C. de Leon, J. Misra and I. W. Martin, eds., *The New Handbook of Political Sociology*. Cambridge: Cambridge University Press, pp 53–78.

Puche i Moré, C. (2013). "The Institute for Catalan Studies and International Women's Day, 2006–2013." *Contributions to Science*, 9, 107–108.

Pullum, A. (2020). "The Dual Nature of Teachers' Unions." *Sociology Compass*, 14, 1–12.

Ramírez Gallegos, F. (2011). "Fragmentación, Reflujo y Descontento. Movimientos Sociales y Cambio Politico en el Ecuador (2000–2010)." In M. Modonesi and J. Rebón, eds., *Una década en movimiento: luchas populares en América Latina en el amanecer del siglo XXI, Colección Perspectivas*. Ciudad de Buenos Aires: CLACSO, pp. 69–106.

Raventós, C. (2018). *Mi corazón dice NO: el movimiento de oposición al TLC en Costa Rica*. San José: Universidad de Costa Rica.

Ray, R. (2000). *Fields of protest: Women's movements in India*. Minneapolis: University of Minnesota Press.

Reese, E. (2011). *They Say Cutback, We Say Fight Back!: Welfare Activism in an Era of Retrenchment*. New York: Russell Sage Foundation.

Reese, E., Petit, C. and Meyer, D. (2010). "Sudden Mobilization: Movement Crossovers, Threats, and the Surprising Rise of the US Antiwar Movement." In *Strategic Alliances: Coalition Building and Social Movements*. Minneapolis: University of Minnesota Press, pp. 266–291.

Reese, E., et al. (2015). "Surveys of World Social Forum Participants Show Influence of Place and Base in the Global Public Sphere." In J. Smith, S. Byrd, E. Reese and E. Smythe, eds., *Handbook on World Social Forum Activism*. Boulder, CO: Paradigm, pp. 64–84.

Riquelme, Q. (2004). "Los Conflictos Sociales en el Contexto de la Democracia Paraguaya." In J. Seoane, ed., *Movimientos Sociales y Conflicto en América Latina*. Buenos Aires: CLACSO, pp. 55–72.

Roberts, K. (1998). *Deepening Democracy?: The Modern Left and Social Movements in Chile and Peru*. Stanford, CA: Stanford University Press.

Roberts, K. (2008). "The Mobilization of Opposition to Economic Liberalization." *Annual Review of Political Science*, 11, 327–349.

Roberts, K. (2015). *Changing Course in Latin America: Party Systems in the Neoliberal Era*. Cambridge: Cambridge University Press.

Robinson, J. (2013). *Contested Water: The Struggle Against Water Privatization in the United States and Canada*. Cambridge, MA: MIT Press.

Robinson, W. (2004). *A Theory of Global Capitalism*. Baltimore, MD: Johns Hopkins University Press.

Robinson, W. (2014). *Global Capitalism and the Crisis of Humanity*. New York: Cambridge University Press.

Robinson, W. (2020). *The Global Police State*. London: Pluto Press.

Rossi, F. (2013). "Juggling Multiple Agendas: The Struggle of Trade Unions against National, Continental, and International Neoliberalism in Argentina." In E. Silva, ed., *Transnational Activism and National Movements in Latin America: Bridging the Divide*. New York and London: Routledge, pp. 141–160.

Roussos, K. and Malamidis, H. (2021). "Social Movements and the Commons: A Framework for Understanding Collective Action in Crisis-Ridden Southern Europe." *Mobilization*, 26(3), 359–379.

Sader, E. and Silverstein, K. (1991). *Without Fear of Being Happy: Lula, the Workers' Party and Brazil*. London: Verso.

Sarracino, F. and Mikucka, M. (2017). "Social Capital in Europe from 1990 to 2012: Trends and Convergence." *Social Indicators Research*, 131(1), 407–432.

Scott, J. (1985). *Weapons of the Weak: Everyday Forms of Peasant Resistance*. New Haven, CT: Yale University Press.

Seidman, G. (1994). *Manufacturing militance: Workers' Movements in Brazil and South Africa, 1970–1985*. Berkeley: University of California Press.

Silva, E. (2009). *Challenging Neoliberalism in Latin America*. Cambridge: Cambridge University Press.

Silva, E. (2013). *Transnational Activism and National Movements in Latin America: Bridging the Divide*. New York and London: Routledge.

Silva, E. (2015). "Indigenous People's Movements, Developments, and Politics in Ecuador and Bolivia." In P. Almeida and A. Cordero, eds., *Handbook of Social Movements across Latin America*. New York: Springer, pp.131–144.

Simmons, E. (2016). *Meaningful Resistance: Market Reforms and the Roots of Social Protest in Latin America*. Cambridge: Cambridge University Press.

Smith, J. (2008). *Social Movements for Global Democracy*. Baltimore, MD: Johns Hopkins University Press.

Smith, J. (2020). "Making Other Worlds Possible: The Battle in Seattle in World-Historical Context." *Socialism and Democracy*, 34(1), 114–137.

Smith, J. and Weist, D. (2012). *Social Movements in the World-System: The Politics of Crisis and Transformation*. New York: Russell Sage Foundation.

Snow, D. and Benford, R. (1988). "Ideology, Frame Resonance, and Participant Mobilization." *International Social Movement Research*, 1(1), 197–217.

Snow, D. and Bernatzky, C. (2018). "The Coterminous Rise of Right-Wing Populism and Superfluous Populations." In G. Fitzi, J. Mackert and B. S. Turmer, eds., *Populism and the Crisis of Democracy* vol. 1. New York: Routledge, pp. 130–146.

Snow, D. and Corrigall-Brown, C. (2005). "Falling on Deaf Ears: Confronting the Prospect of Nonresonant Frames." In D. Croteau, W. Hoynes and C. Ryan, eds., *Rhyming Hope and History: Activists, Academics, and Social Movement Scholarship*. Minneapolis: University of Minnesota Press, pp. 222–238.

Snow, D., Cress, D., Downey, L. and Jones, A. (1998). "Disrupting the 'Quotidian': Reconceptualizing the Relationship between Breakdown and the Emergence of Collective Action." *Mobilization*, 3(1), 1–22.

Sobering, K. and Lapegna, P. (2021). "Alternative Organizational Survival: A Comparison of Two Worker-Recuperated Businesses in Buenos Aires, Argentina." *Social Problems*, (00), 1–17.

Somers, M. R. (2008). *Genealogies of Citizenship: Markets, Statelessness, and the Right to Have Rights*. Cambridge: Cambridge University Press.

Somma, N., Bargsted, M., Disi Pavlic, R. and Medel, R. (2021). "No Water in the Oasis: The Chilean Spring of 2019–2020." *Social Movement Studies*, 20 (4), 495–502.

Somma, N., Garreton, M., Campos, T. and Joignant, A. (2020). "Radiografia Del Estallido Social." *Informe Anual Observatorio de Conflictos*, 11–21.

Somma, N. and Medel, R. (2019). "What Makes a Big Demonstration? Exploring the Impact of Mobilization Strategies on the Size of Demonstrations." *Social Movement Studies*, 18(2), 233–251.

Sosa, E. (2013). *Dinámica de la protesta social en Honduras*. Tegucigalpa: Editorial Guaymuras.

Sosa, E. (2019). "Honduras a Diez Años Del Golpe de Estado: El Presidente Juan Orlando Hernández En Llamas." *Nuestra America*, 33, 8–10.

Staggenborg, S. (1986). "Coalition Work in the Pro-Choice Movement: Organizational and Environmental Opportunities and Obstacles." *Social Problems*, 33(5), 374–390.

Staggenborg, S. (2022). *Social Movements*. Oxford: Oxford University Press.

Staggenborg, S. and Lecomte, J. (2009). "Social Movement Campaigns: Mobilization and Outcomes in the Montreal Women's Movement Community." *Mobilization: An International Quarterly*, 14(2), 163–180.

Standing, G. (2011). *The Precariat: The New Dangerous Class*. London: Bloomsbury.

Tarrow, S. (1989). *Democracy and Disorder: Protest and Politics in Italy, 1965–1974*. New York: Oxford University Press.

Tarrow, S. (2021). *Movements and Parties: Critical Connections in American Political Development*. Cambridge: Cambridge University Press.

Tilly, C. (1978). *From Mobilization to Revolution*. Reading: Addison-Wesley.

Tilly, C. (1999). "From Interactions to Outcomes in Social Movements." In M. Giugni, D. McAdam and C. Tilly, eds., *How Social Movements Matter*. Minneapolis: University of Minnesota Press, pp. 253–270.

Tilly, C. (2004). *Social Movements, 1768–2004*. Boulder, CO: Paradigm.

Torres Santana, A. and Pérez Martín, A. (2021). "Editors' Introduction to the Dossier Feminist and LGTBIQ+ Repertoires: Collective Action and Struggle for Rights." *Revista Temas Sociológicos*, 29, 27–37.

Trejo, G. (2012). *Popular Movements in Autocracies: Religion, Repression, and Indigenous Collective Action in Mexico*. Cambridge: Cambridge University Press.

Tufekci, Z. (2017). *Twitter and Tear Gas: The Power and Fragility of Networks Protest*. New Haven, CT: Yale University Press.

Tversky, A. and Kahneman, D. (1992). "Advances in Prospect Theory: Cumulative Representation of Uncertainty." *Journal of Risk and Uncertainty*, 5(4), 297–323.

United Press International (UPI) (1983). *Police and demonstrators clash in Acapulco*, https://advance.lexis.com/api/document?collection=news&id=urn:contentItem:3SJB-F420-001X-R454-00000-00&context=1516831.

Useem, B. and Goldstone, J. (2022). "The Paradox of Victory: Social Movement Fields, Adverse Outcomes, and Social Movement Success." *Theory and Society*, 51, 31–60.

Van Cott, D. (2007). *From Movements to Parties in Latin America: The Evolution of Ethnic Politics*. Cambridge: Cambridge University Press.

Van Dyke, N. and Amos, B. (2017). "Social Movement Coalitions: Formation, Longevity, and Success." *Sociology Compass*, 11(7), e12489.

Vasi, I. and Suh, C. (2016). "Online Activities, Spatial Proximity, and the Diffusion of the Occupy Wall Street Movement in the United States." *Mobilization: An International Quarterly*, 21(2), 139–154.

Von Bulow, M. (2010). *Building Transnational Networks: Civil Society and the Politics of Trade in the Americas*. New York: Cambridge University Press.

Wacquant, L. (2009). *Punishing the Poor: The Neoliberal Government of Social Insecurity*. Durham, NC: Duke University Press.

Waghre, P. (2021). "'Radically Networked Societies: The Case of the Farmers' Protests in India.'" *Indian Public Policy Review*, 2(3), 41–64.

Walton, J. and Seddon, D. (1994). *Free Markets [and] Food Riots: The Politics of Global Adjustment*. Oxford: Blackwell.

Williamson, J. (1993). "Democracy and the 'Washington consensus.'" *World Development*, 21(8), 1329–1336.

Wood, L. (2012). *Direct Action, Deliberation, and Diffusion: Collective Action after the WTO Protests in Seattle*. Cambridge: Cambridge University Press.

World Bank. 2022. *International Debt Statistics 2022*. Washington, DC: World Bank.

Zepeda-Millán, C. (2017). *Latino Mass Mobilization: Immigration, Racialization, and Activism*. Cambridge: Cambridge University Press.

Cambridge Elements

Contentious Politics

About the Series

Cambridge Elements series in Contentious Politics provides an important opportunity to bridge research and communication about the politics of protest across disciplines and between the academy and a broader public. Our focus is on political engagement, disruption, and collective action that extends beyond the boundaries of conventional institutional politics. Social movements, revolutionary campaigns, organized reform efforts, and more or less spontaneous uprisings are the important and interesting developments that animate contemporary politics; we welcome studies and analyses that promote better understanding and dialogue.

Cambridge Elements

Contentious Politics

Elements in the series

The Phantom at The Opera: Social Movements and Institutional Politics
Sidney Tarrow

Contested Legitimacy in Ferguson: Nine Hours on Canfield Drive
Joshua Bloom

The Street and the Ballot Box: Interactions Between Social Movements and Electoral Politics in Authoritarian Contexts
Lynette H. Ong

Collective Resistance to Neoliberalism
Paul Almeida & Amalia Pérez Martín

Progressive Social Movements in the Pandemics Crisis
Donatella Della Porta

A full series listing is available at: www.cambridge.org/ECTP

Printed in the United States
by Baker & Taylor Publisher Services